MARY

THE MOTHER OF JESUS

Dr. Ana Méndez Ferrell

Voice of The Light Ministries

DEDICATION

I dedicate this book to my dear Heavenly Father, to whom I owe all things, and to Jesus Christ, my savior who brought me out of darkness and revealed His light to me. I will always be thankful for giving me His Spirit, his wisdom, health, and all the riches of His glory to share His love and power with others.

Voice of The Light Ministries

MARY, THE MOTHER OF JESUS
2016 Copyright © Ana Méndez Ferrell

Category   Deliverance

Publisher   Voice of The Light Ministries
P.O. Box 3418
Ponte Vedra, Florida, 32004
United States of America

www.VoiceOfTheLight.com

ISBN 978-1-933163-84-0

CONTENTS

INTRODUCTION

God in His grace and mercy has granted me many spiritual experiences through which I have known Him and loved Him deeply.

I have also been blessed with powerful angelic visitations. In 1975 I was one of the witnesses who saw the apparition of the Virgin of Garabandal in Spain.

I'm writing this book with much affection for those who love God and seek His ways and blessing, for Catholics and all Christian denominations.

I was born into a catholic home. At the age of 29, after a transforming encounter with Jesus Christ, I completely dedicated my life to Him. From that moment on, I became a student of the Holy Scriptures and history. Years later I obtained a Doctorate degree in Theology from the *Latin University of Theology in California.*

All this brought me to an understanding of the spiritual realm to discern both the blessings and dangers found in it. Not only is there heaven, light and the many wonders surrounding God, but there are also dark regions where satan and his army fight to govern the earth and to hinder God's works.

Many people have had mystical and supernatural experiences, but it's very important to be able to discern exactly who is producing these experiences - God or the devil.

lucifer was the archangel of all beauty and wisdom until he was caught up in iniquity. He wanted to sit on the holy mountain of God to be like the Almighty. His name means *beautiful light* and he was just like his name states, amazingly bright and gleaming.

He knew the ways of the Lord. He became an expert imitator and a master of deception, but he is the counterfeit. The counterfeit is not the real thing; however, it can look almost exactly as the real one. For example, a counterfeit US$100 bill - if it's really good looks exactly like the genuine one and only expert eyes and hands are able to detect that it's fake.

Make no mistake. satan is like that counterfeit US$100 bill. He lost all authority when Christ defeated him on the cross of Calvary. The only power he has is the ability to make us fall into his traps by creating the most unbelievable deceptions.

God, on the other hand, has placed eternity in the heart of man. He has also given us the desire to seek Him and feel His presence.

He has made everything beautiful in its time. Also He has put eternity in their hearts, except that no one can find out the work that God does from beginning to end.

Ecclesiastes 3:11

One way or another, man knows there is something more beyond this life and all civilizations have searched for it by invoking all kinds of spirits and pagan gods. All cultures originated from a *cult* or form of worship offered to a spiritual entity that revealed itself to them. Now, more than ever, there is a hunger and thirst to discover and explore the supernatural world, but if the right way is not known, the consequence is spiritual death.

All the ways of a man are pure in his own eyes
But the Lord weighs the spirits.

Proverbs 16:2

There is a way that seems right to a man,
But its end is the way of death.

Proverbs 14:12

satan's goal is to divert man's attention towards him and he will do it through glorious apparitions of false angels of light.

And no wonder! For Satan himself transforms himself into an angel of light. Therefore it is no great thing if his ministers also transform themselves into ministers of righteousness, whose end will be according to their works.

2 Corinthians 11:14-15

Seeing a false angel of light or a real one is something that goes far beyond our understanding. If we don't have discernment and are not anchored in the truth of God and His ways, it's very easy to be deceived. If we allow ourselves to get carried away by its beauty and brightness, we are easy prey, but God in His word gives us guidelines for knowing who is actually appearing to us.

God has used many angelic apparitions to announce messages, but not everything that shines is from heaven or comes from God. The purpose of this book is to guide you, beloved reader, and to place the tools of discernment and wisdom in your hands so you will understand how to analyze an apparition and its message.

I also want you to really know the message that Mary, the mother of our Lord, left us through her exemplary life and her love for the Father and Son, and from what was written about her in the Bible.

CHAPTER 1
MY ENCOUNTER WITH THE VIRGIN OF GARABANDAL

Born into a Catholic Home

I was born in Mexico City and grew up in a Catholic home. My father was a devout Catholic.

Unfortunately, under very painful circumstances, my family was torn apart when I was 9 years old. My mother raised us and my father convinced her to send us to private Catholic schools. We learned to fully devote ourselves to the Lord. We developed a life of prayer and went on spiritual retreats because we lived according to faith principles. Because of this foundation, I always had a hunger to truly seek God.

Over the years, the church became my place of refuge. Some days I spent the entire afternoon inside the sanctuary meditating on the Lord. The cross always amazed me. It really hurt me to see the images of my beloved Jesus hanging dead, with His body covered in blood. I didn't understand why we always had to see Him like that because His resurrection is the true result.

I loved seeing Him alive. I found comfort in imagining Him in His glory next to His Father. Seeing Him this way affirmed my faith, at least for a moment and then I returned to my sad reality. He was up there and I was down here. My biggest pain was not being able to get to Him. Like many, I felt unworthy and sinful.

In 1975 my twin sister and I lived in Paris. We were only 19 years old and lived from hand-to-mouth in a studio apartment. My sister, Mercedes worked in a small corner of the studio preparing her journalism notes.

We didn't always have enough money to buy food, but I cooked when there was something to cook. There were weeks when our daily diet consisted of only a tomato on a piece of bread and some yogurt. Since I was just there as a tourist, I didn't have a work permit. This made it very difficult for me to work and my sister's salary was barely enough to pay rent on the studio. Some months we had just enough money and some months we were blessed with a little bit left over.

I trusted that God wouldn't abandon me and He didn't. Because I had a talent for horseback riding I was able to find a job at an equestrian club. My job was to clean the stables and help train horses. As much as this was a blessing, I faced the terrible rejection Parisians have towards Mexicans and Latin Americans. Being Mexican made it truly a difficult cross to bear. One day, however, we received a phone call from a dear friend who invited us to her grandparents' home in Spain for the summer. They offered to cover all expenses while we were there, which made her invitation irresistible.

We were excited and managed to save money to make the trip to Madrid. Their house was a colonial mansion built on rock. The house was large and had many wonderfully decorated bedrooms. I was grateful I was given my own room. This was paradise considering the conditions we lived under in Paris. Our friend was a lot of fun and she had many cousins and friends that quickly joined us. We made plans every day to visit the museums, walk the streets of the beautiful capital and have a great time eating out.

Our plan was to have a great time in the "motherland" I longed to know, but an encounter was awaiting me that I couldn't begin to imagine.

It was on the second or third night while I was sleeping peacefully when suddenly a glimmering light woke me up. My mind couldn't believe what I saw. Before me was an extraordinary vision. It was a woman radiating light. Her face was so beautiful. It was so full of tenderness and mercy that it captivated my soul. Her hair was blonde and wavy and went down to the back of her knees. It moved like waves of light similar to when hair is under water. Her dress was white and her tunic was light blue with a gold trim. Her dress and tunic were shining like twinkling stars. I was speechless, more admiring her than observing her. Then she spoke to me. Her voice was so sincere and gentle it pierced my soul.

"I am the virgin and I have come because I have a message for you that I want you to take to the world. You must come to Garabandal."

When she finished speaking she started to disappear. "I have to go where? Don't leave! Please repeat the name of the place, Gara… what?" I asked in desperation, because I didn't catch the name of the place.

But she disappeared without saying another word. I cried out to her. I desperately wanted her to return and tell me the name of the place, but she didn't come back. I didn't sleep at all that night. I closed my eyes and opened them again and again hoping I would see her. I finally fell asleep at around daybreak.

When they called me down to breakfast, everyone noticed there was something different about me. They couldn't explain it, but everyone commented. I told them what happened, along with my frustration of not hearing the name of the place correctly. We searched the map for towns and cities that began with "Gara", but we couldn't find anything.

I was frustrated. I felt I let her down. How many people have actually seen the virgin? So few! And I, the least worthy of all, didn't hear what she said.

That day I didn't feel like going anywhere because I was so upset. When evening came, I went to my room brokenhearted, but with the hope the virgin would have compassion and reappear. I prayed the rosary. After asking her to come back I closed my eyes and fell asleep.

It was around 3:00 a.m. when I felt a presence that ran through my whole body. I saw the glimmering light. I couldn't help but cry from the excitement. I was so happy!

"Don't worry, I am your Mother and I will not leave you; I came to tell you I had a message for you and I will make sure you make it to the right place. You have to go to Garabandal. I will be waiting there for you."

"I will be there," I said. My voice was trembling from the privilege of hearing her voice. After I said that I'd be there, she disappeared.

This time I listened carefully and I wrote down the name of the place, so I wouldn't forget it.

The next morning I went down to breakfast and I told everyone about the second apparition. Everyone looked at me in a strange way.

"What are you going to do?" My sister asked. "We already looked at the map and there is no place that even comes close to sounding like the word you mentioned."

"The truth is I don't know what I'm going to do, but if she wants me to go the place she'll make sure I get there," I answered.

My vacation ended after that. I stopped participating in activities with everyone and spent my time praying. Five nights in a row she appeared to me telling me the same thing. I decided to go to the Curia (governing church officials) in Madrid and ask if anyone knew something about Garabandal.

A friendly priest welcomed me. I believe his name was Francisco, but I don't exactly remember. When I told him what happened and that I saw the virgin his face was transformed. It was as if I was giving him a confirmation of something churning within him.

He said to me, "You must speak to one of the priests; he knows everything there is to know about that place. As a matter of fact, he's already been there." He called for the other priest and a heavy-set man with a big smile came running into the room.

"Did the virgin appear to you too? That's wonderful! I had the same experience and I went there. The virgin is appearing to a lot of people. You are very fortunate!" He said.

"Why me?" I asked.

"I don't know, she is the one who chooses and we must obey," He replied.

He took me to a library inside the building where he pulled out a map and drew the route to Garabandal. The place didn't even appear on the map. This was 1976. It wasn't like what we have today with Google earth to find obscure places. At that time, we didn't even have personal computers.

Garabandal was just a tiny hamlet of 15 houses. There weren't any roads leading directly there. You had to get there from the nearest road and hiking up through the mountains.

Fig. 1 — Santiago de Garabandal

The journey to Garabandal was a real challenge because I hardly had a cent left. But faith and youth open all doors and this one was definitely not going to close. I said goodbye to everyone and went to the train station. I needed to get out of the city and then my only alternative was to hitchhike.

The train dropped me off in the first town north of Madrid. I needed to take the road to Avila and then on to Burgos. I left the train station in the blistering summer heat in central Spain. The sun was bright and the temperature was about 105° Fahrenheit *(40,5° Celsius)*. There wasn't a single tree near the road where I could rest under the shade.

I was very young and innocent and didn't recognize danger very well back then. Beyond that, my blind faith pushed me to confront anything as long as I made it to where the virgin was waiting for me. I was certain she would make sure I arrived and that was enough for me.

Soon, a truck came along and the driver offered me a ride, but after about an hour he began making improper advances. I realized the horrible circumstances I was in by accepting the ride.

I started to think about how to escape. I remained calm and when the truck slowed down I jumped out, suitcase and all. The man was probably afraid I would report him and he sped off down the road.

I hurt all over, but by the grace of God I didn't break one single bone. I picked up my suitcase, but I was very sore and my arm was covered in blood. I sat next to the road. After a while another truck carrying watermelons stopped.

When the driver saw I was hurt, he quickly tried to help me. The driver was a very friendly old man. He helped me wash my scrapes and scratches - some of which were pretty deep. He gave me water to drink and some warm watermelon to eat.

He said, "This is outrageous! There are some very bad people around here. You must be careful. I'm headed to Burgos and I can take you if you want. Don't worry, I like helping people and you will be safe with me."

I didn't have many alternatives and the old man made me feel comfortable. And he just happened to be headed in the same direction I needed to go. I climbed up into the truck and continued on my journey. Because he really wanted to help me, he ended up going out of his way to drop me off at the place where I needed to start climbing the mountain to Garabandal.

Another Supernatural Episode

Climbing the mountain wasn't easy. It was very steep and I had to follow a very narrow path that was trampled with the footprints from animals and from the people who lived in the little town. Carrying a suitcase after being hurt earlier made the journey even more difficult.

When I arrived at the tiny hamlet, I realized there wasn't a single hotel or boarding house. It was almost nightfall and I was concerned if someone didn't offer me a place to stay I would be in serious trouble. I knocked on the first door. An old woman around 70 years old opened the door. She was short and had a smile from ear-to-ear that lit up her entire face.

"Ah, it's you. It's great that you have arrived … please come in. Your room is ready and dinner is hot … because I assume you must be very hungry." The woman said this as if I was a relative she had been expecting.

Fig. 2 — My little house in Garabandal

"Excuse me. I believe you must be confused." I said to her. "I don't know who you are expecting, but I'm just a tourist coming to see the virgin and I need a place to stay."

"No my dear, it's you who I've been waiting for," she said. "The virgin appeared to me and showed me your face and told me when you would arrive. So, please come in. Everything is ready."

I was really puzzled. What place was this? What was awaiting me? I was speechless as the woman took me to my room. It was a very comfortable room with a rustic country feel decorated with a crocheted bedspread and hand-knitted cushions.

We spoke for hours during dinner about the apparitions and messages from the virgin. She appeared frequently between 1961 and 1965 to four young girls from San Sebastian of Garabandal, but on occasion, she appeared to several others like me from different parts of the world.

During our conversation she took me outside to show me where the virgin would appear. It was summer and the sun doesn't set until around 10:00 p.m. so it was easy to see the place. It wasn't a very big mountain. It was close to the hamlet and I saw tall pine trees at the top. She pointed to three specific pine trees where the virgin chose to speak to people. You had to go there early, around 6:30 a.m. or 7:00 a.m. after praying the rosary at 5:00 a.m., or in the afternoon after the 6:00 p.m. rosary.

Fig. 3 — Pine woods where the virgin would appear

I hardly slept that night. I was counting the minutes until I could have another encounter with the virgin, but for two days nothing happened. I went to a tiny church where the people from the town gathered to pray. I joined them hoping to increase my chances of another encounter with the virgin.

On the third day in the afternoon, I went up to the pine woods when no one else was around. I waited in silence. A strange sensation ran through my body. It was like a warm breeze under my clothes and I felt as if I were in a trance. I was there, but at the same time I wasn't. I saw her again and she gave me this message:

"There will be a great Miracle — a sign that will be seen by all my children. I will bring them to this place from all over the world and I will speak to them. I know the day and the hour of the end. I will let them know eight days ahead so they can come. I promise I will be with you until the end of time. You will be with me during the end of the world and after you will join me in the glory of paradise. A great punishment will come upon the earth. That is why you must do good works and constantly pray the rosary. This must be propagated for the salvation of sinners and for the preservation of humanity from the terrible punishment that the good God is threatening it with. Constantly pray and I will listen and I will respond to your petitions. Make many sacrifices and penitence and don't forget about the Holy Eucharist. Always think about the sacrifices of my Son."

That afternoon as I stood in the pine woods listening to the message, I wrote down every word because I didn't want to forget any of it. When I came down the mountain I felt as if I was flying. I couldn't wait to tell the old woman about my experience. When I told her what happened she was very happy and she gave me one of the rosaries the virgin had kissed.

"She has kissed many objects and they become miraculous. Here, I want you to have this one," the woman said as she gave me the antique rosary.

I spent long hours in front of the pine trees interceding for the world and for my family, but that was the only time I saw the virgin. Because I didn't have another encounter, I finally decided that the mission was complete and it was now time to return to Madrid.

Later in this book I will describe how God helped me to discern and process this experience. But first, I want you to meet Mary, the Mother of our Lord.

CHAPTER 2
RETURNING TO HISTORY

Mary is one of the most important characters in the Bible because she was chosen to carry the Messiah in her womb, but she is also one of the least understood.

In different churches and denominations that profess to be Christian, her name and personality have been portrayed either total exaltation or complete disdain. No other saint from the Old Testament or the New Testament is treated with so much ambiguity.

This is because two very different Marys exist. One is the mother of our Lord and the other one comes from different pagan cultures. The "false" Mary cleverly takes the name of the virgin with the purpose of deceiving believers and diverting their faith. These two maternal figures - the *real* Mary and the *false* Mary - have been mixed throughout the ages which has created a great deal of confusion.

It's important to look at the history and origin of many "common" beliefs during these difficult times when spirituality and faith in the hearts of many are fading. We have simply come to accept some things out of tradition, because that's how we were taught. We never questioned if these things were in accordance with our Heavenly Father's heart.

God is once again putting things in order. He wants us to clearly see His ways and come close to Him in the fullness and blessings He has for each and every one of us.

Cultural Background of Mary, the Mother of Our Lord

In order to truly understand historic figures, it's imperative to look back at the cultural background, such as the era in which the person lived and the circumstances that surrounded them. The most accurate document that will lead us to know the true Mary, the mother of our Lord, is without a doubt *the Bible*.

The Old Testament from beginning to end prophesied the coming of the Messiah, the Savior of the world. His name was Emmanuel, which means God with us and Yeshua which means Jesus the Savior, in Hebrew. The birth, life, death and resurrection of the Son of God is not only the main topic of the Judeo-Christian Scriptures, but also the most important event in history. If it weren't for the coming and triumph of our Savior Jesus Christ, the world would have continued to be lost and without hope and basing itself on pagan philosophies and religions. Jesus came to save the world and this is the core of His message and His work.

God didn't choose a nation among the existing ones on earth to announce and bring forth His Son. He created a nation for Himself. He called Abraham, who lived in the city of Ur of the Chaldeans, to leave his country and his family. Through God's divine plan, Abraham and his wife Sarah in their old age conceived and gave birth to a son named Isaac. The nation of Israel emerged from this seed. God needed to form a nation that would keep His laws and announce the coming of His Son, the Messiah. God raised great men, kings and prophets from this nation who feared and honored His holy name and who made sure His law prevailed.

Although there weren't always just and righteous people in the history of the Jewish nation, God always made sure there was a holy remnant that would cause the nation to turn back to God.

God raised up Isaiah from among the prophets. He was the first to prophesy what the coming of the Messiah would be like.

> *Therefore the Lord Himself will give you a sign: Behold, the virgin shall conceive and bear a Son, and shall call His name Immanuel.*
>
> *Isaiah 7:14*

God would choose a virgin from among His people to be the vessel to carry the Son of God in her womb. What a great honor for the woman chosen for this task! But what would this be like? What did God see in her?

God had to choose someone according to His heart, totally holy and obedient to the law He gave through Moses. The chosen virgin had to have a strong character. She had to be extremely humble to not take any glory from the future Messiah. She would no doubt be tempted in that sense. It's very easy for human nature to want to exalt itself due to a great achievement or recognition such as, "the mother of the Son of God." Mary would have to know how to stay strong *and* humble before this glorious calling.

satan always tempted the people of Israel with the sin that most offended God - "idolatry". There is no greater abomination mentioned in the Holy Scriptures than men giving glory to paintings and figurines made from wood, iron or stone.

Mary knew this well. As a faithful Jewish woman she attended synagogue every Saturday for training and instruction in the law of God. She was a woman of profound knowledge of the Torah

(Jewish law), the Psalms, the Prophets and she feared The Lord. We see in the scriptures that she obeyed the law and purified herself on the Day of Atonement, like any other woman.

> *Now when the days of her (Mary) purification according to the law of Moses were completed, they brought Him to Jerusalem to present Him to the Lord (as it is written in the law of the Lord, "Every male who opens the womb shall be called holy to the Lord"), and to offer a sacrifice according to what is said in the law of the Lord, "A pair of turtledoves or two young pigeons.[1]*
>
> *Luke 2:22-24*

Obeying the word and the law of God were undeniable conditions God saw choosing Mary by His grace.

The Word that Resonated in Mary's Heart

Mary heard rabbis and priests citing passages all of her life that affirmed her heart in justice and righteousness, detesting all types of idolatry and sin.

The knowledge of the law and the ways that God established for His people are very important to understand in order to determine the intimate thoughts of Mary and her subsequent message to humanity.

> *Speak to the children of Israel, saying: 'If a woman has conceived, and borne a male child, then she shall be unclean seven days; as in the days of her customary impurity she shall be unclean."*
>
> *Leviticus 12:2*

---

[1] *After giving birth Jewish women had to bring an animal to be sacrificed by the priest in order to be purified. The Jewish law considered a woman on her period or after giving birth to be unclean.*

When the days of her purification are fulfilled, whether for a son or a daughter, she shall bring to the priest a lamb of the first year as a burnt offering, and a young pigeon or a turtledove as a sin offering, to the door of the tabernacle of meeting. Then he shall offer it before the Lord, and make atonement for her. And she shall be clean from the flow of her blood. This is the law for her who has borne a male or a female.

Leviticus 12:6-7

The Jewish Law

Let's look at some portions of the Jewish law to help us understand the thoughts of the *real* Mary, which are radically opposed to those of her imposter, "the *false* Mary."

You shall have no other gods before Me.

"You shall not make for yourself a carved image — any likeness of anything that is in heaven above, or that is in the earth beneath, or that is in the water under the earth; you shall not bow down to them nor serve them. For I, the Lord your God, am a jealous God, visiting the iniquity of the fathers upon the children to the third and fourth generations of those who hate Me, but showing mercy to thousands, to those who love Me and keep My commandments.

Exodus 20:3-6

"Thus says the Lord, the King of Israel,
And his Redeemer, the Lord of hosts:
'I am the First and I am the Last;
Besides Me there is no God.

Those who make an image, all of them are useless,
And their precious things shall not profit;
They are their own witnesses;
They neither see nor know, that they may be ashamed.
Who would form a god or mold an image
That profits him nothing?

He falls down before it and worships it,
Prays to it and says,
"Deliver me, for you are my god!"

Isaiah 44:6,9,10,17b

I am the Lord, that is My name;
And My glory I will not give to another,
Nor My praise to carved images.

Isaiah 42:8

Mary the Mother of Our Lord knew these words perfectly well along with others found in the scriptures that describe idolatry as the greatest abomination to God. Being holy and chosen, she would never broadcast a message that would lead the people of God to worship her or to create carved images and paintings to honor her.

Later in this book, we will look at how the *false* Mary infiltrated the Church to position herself as the center of worship.

The Law Against Invoking the Dead

Mary grew up hearing The Law and the history of Israel and the events that cost the lives of some chosen men of God, because they transgressed His law. She would never invite anyone to invoke *her* presence after she departed this world and went on to be in the presence of The Lord. This would mean doing something against the commandments of God and she would never be a part of something like that.

> *A man or a woman who is a medium (one who invokes the dead)[2], or who has familiar spirits, shall surely be put to death; they shall stone them with stones. Their blood shall be upon them.'*
>
> *Leviticus 20:27*

Invoking a spirit was a pagan practice which King Saul[3] committed by invoking the spirit of the Prophet Samuel, who had already died. This caused God to despise him and destroy his kingdom giving it over to death (1 Samuel 28:7-19).

The Prophecies

Since the fall of man in the Garden of Eden, the Father prophesied the plan of salvation through His only Son Jesus. He cursed the serpent announcing how the seed would come from the woman and crush the serpent's head destroying all his empire.

---

[2] *Explanation in parenthesis written by author.*

[3] *King Saul, first king of Israel*

So the Lord God said to the serpent:
"Because you have done this,
You are cursed more than all cattle,
And more than every beast of the field;
On your belly you shall go,
And you shall eat dust
All the days of your life.
And I will put enmity
Between you and the woman,
And between your seed and her Seed;
He shall crush your head,
And you shall bruise His heel."

Genesis 3:14-15

In this scripture we see how a terrible enmity surges between the devil and the woman as a consequence of the curse. satan thought he obtained total dominion of the earth when he caused Adam and Eve to fall into transgression, but God already had a plan to reconcile His creation to Himself.

There were probably times when Mary listened to the teachers of the law talk about this enmity. Certainly in her childhood and adolescence, God placed thoughts in her heart as well as circumstances in her life that formed her into a woman of great valor and emotional resistance. Mary was a woman with extraordinary faith capable of taking steps in her walk with God that many wouldn't dare take.

One of these great tests had to do with the supernatural conception of the Son of God. It was not going to be easy to face society in those days as an unmarried pregnant woman.

Nowadays, it's easy to say that Jesus was born of a virgin, but in those days no one would believe that He came from the Holy Spirit. God even sent an angel — probably Gabriel, the same angel that brought Mary the tidings of the conception — to bring peace and confirmation to Joseph since it was not easy for him to grasp.

Jewish law was very severe when it came to immorality and the intimate union between a man and a woman outside of marriage, especially when it involved a priesthood lineage. In this case, Mary was the daughter of Eli, from the family of the Aaronic priesthood.

> *The daughter of any priest, if she profanes herself by playing the harlot, she profanes her father. She shall be burned with fire.*
>
> *Leviticus 21:9*

Mary knew that if a woman conceived a child outside of marriage she would immediately be singled out, rejected and if no one redeemed her she would undoubtedly die. Because of this law, Mary had a life-challenging decision to make. She could choose loving her life and her reputation more or she could choose the will of God. God would use this to test her faith, which would either qualify her as the mother of the Messiah or disqualify her for loving her life and reputation more than the will of God.

CHAPTER 3
The Character &
The Message of Mary

As I touched on in the previous chapter — finding truth and grasping it — requires knowing the origin and authenticity of the documents we base our faith on. In order to fully understand who Mary was and to form a principle based on truth, we need to rely on the Bible as a sacred document. Relying on what someone said, on tradition or on uncertain documents will undoubtedly lead us to something erroneous.

The Bible, on the other hand, is absolutely trustworthy and has been preserved throughout generations. As we search the Bible, we can find what God wants us to know about the mother of Jesus.

I believe, and it's inferred throughout scripture, that Mary knew in her heart that her calling and mission in life was of great importance. For instance, during the announcement she didn't even react to the fact that there was an angel appearing before her.

What surprises Mary more than the apparition itself, is the greeting. When the angel Gabriel declares the supernatural conception of Jesus, Mary is surprised to hear the description of how it would happen, not that it would happen. Let's analyze this crucial moment in more detail.

The Announcement

Now in the sixth month the angel Gabriel was sent by God to a city of Galilee named Nazareth, to a virgin betrothed to a man whose name was Joseph, of the house of David. The virgin's name was Mary. And having come in, the angel said to her, "Rejoice, highly favored one, the Lord is with you; blessed are you among women!"

But when she saw him, she was troubled at his saying, and considered what manner of greeting this was. Then the angel said to her, "Do not be afraid, Mary, for you have found favor with God. And behold, you will conceive in your womb and bring forth a Son, and shall call His name JESUS. He will be great, and will be called the Son of the Highest; and The Lord God will give Him the throne of His father David. And He will reign over the house of Jacob forever, and of His Kingdom there will be no end."

Then Mary said to the angel, "How can this be, since I do not know a man?"

Luke 1:26-34

Notice that Mary didn't ask a single question regarding her being the chosen vessel. There is not one bit of doubt. Also, she didn't assume that the child would come after she married Joseph. She simply asked how this supernatural event would take place.

This is a great teaching for all of us. When God announces something or determines our calling in life, our response should always be with a grateful and expectant heart knowing that what God tells us, He will actually do.

And the angel answered and said to her, "The Holy Spirit will come upon you, and the power of the Highest will overshadow you; therefore, also, that Holy One who is to be born will be called the Son of God. Now indeed, Elizabeth your relative has also conceived a son in her old age; and this is now the sixth month for her who was called barren. For with God nothing will be impossible."

Then Mary said, "Behold the maidservant of the Lord! Let it be to me according to your word." And the angel departed from her.

Luke 1:35-38

Mary's response is a great example for us. When we read the Bible, or hear the sweet voice of The Holy Spirit and learn the great things God has promised us we can also respond with a humble heart: *Let it be to me according to your word.*

From the moment of this announcement we can see a great deal about Mary's personality and behavior. Mary's response, *"Let it be to me according to your word"* demonstrates her character. As I said before, Mary was a woman of great courage and faith. We can learn much from her.

Not only was it the most extraordinary calling, it was a calling that brought rejection and persecution from the Jewish society of her time. The terrible enmity previously announced would come upon her from the devil and could cause her death.

But Mary knew God had chosen her and He would take care of everything else.

When Mary heard the announcement she began to sing a joyful song. The song can be broken down into three parts.

At the beginning we can appreciate the extraordinary aspects of her personality and upbringing.

In the second part we see her exalting God. It's interesting to see which aspects of The Almighty she focuses on in this part. They are obviously the ones God has increased in her life.

The third part has to do with the prophetic aspect of her mission and ministry, and how she recognizes the authority of the written Word of God.

Part 1 — Her Personality

*And Mary said: "My soul magnifies the Lord, And my spirit has rejoiced in **God my Savior**. For He has regarded the lowly state of His maidservant; For behold, henceforth all generations will call me blessed.*

Luke 1:46-48

In this part of the song we can see Mary's heart, which God saw when choosing her. She doesn't feel grand, nor does she exalt herself, nor does she look for worship or fame. She recognizes what all humanity should recognize — that we all need a Savior and He is God made flesh, our Messiah.

Mary was humble like no other. This is the virtue God needed to see in the woman who would carry His only Son in her womb. God knew the devil would tempt Mary just like he did the first woman with something succulent and delicious that filled her with exaltation and disqualified her.

From the moment of the fall, Adam's wife Eve believed the lying, seductive words of satan that filled her with pride. It caused her to follow the words of the devil instead of the commandments of God.

"... For God knows that in the day you eat of it your eyes will be opened, and you will be like God, knowing good and evil."

So when the woman saw that the tree was good for food, that it was pleasant to the eyes, and a tree desirable to make one wise, she took of its fruit and ate. She also gave to her husband with her, and he ate.

Genesis 3:5-6

satan's strategy to tempt Mary would probably be along those same lines. He would promise her the power to be like God, to exalt herself above her own Son, and to steal His Glory and purpose and turn the world's attention to her. However, she feared God and she was faithful and just in all her ways.

She would never have given in to such temptation or deception.

Notice in the second part of her song to God, how Mary's message is always to exalt and worship God and to lead all generations to fear the holy name of The Eternal Father. Her message is always to direct humanity to recognize the Power of The Father above all things and to be humble before God.

Mary, the *real* mother of Jesus didn't seek to stand alongside the powerful, nor did she seek crowns to exalt herself. The message she left us leads us to the foot of the Cross and to Jesus Christ, to the life of service, to selflessness, compassion and love for others. She knew the reward of the humble and the punishment of those who seek their own glory.

Part 2 — Mary Exalts God

For He who is mighty has done great things for me, And holy is His name. And His mercy is on those who fear Him From generation to generation.

He has shown strength with His arm; He has scattered the proud in the imagination of their hearts. He has put down the mighty from their thrones, And exalted the lowly. He has filled the hungry with good things, And the rich He has sent away empty.

Luke 1:49-53

Here we see that as she lifts up The Father, she proclaims the Mercy of God over those who fear Him. She knows in her humble heart how much God despises those who exalt themselves and enthrone themselves to be worshiped. She knows God is pleased and exalts with those who are low and meek. This one of they key messages she left us in the Scriptures, and a real example of who she truly is.

Part 3 — She recognizes the Authority of the written Word of God

He has helped His servant Israel, In remembrance of His mercy, As He spoke to our fathers, To Abraham and to his seed forever."

Luke 1:49-55

Mary is thankful and recognizes the fulfillment of the prophecies given to her fathers, which are the anchor of her mission and ministry. Here we see that she is not ignorant of the Scriptures, but rather she was able to discern who was that precious seed that had been promised to Abraham. Note that she speaks about a seed and not seeds as if there were many, but only one in which the whole world was going to be blessed, her son Jesus Christ.

The Birth of the Messiah

"So it was, that while they were there, the days were completed for her to be delivered. And she brought forth her firstborn Son, and wrapped Him in swaddling cloths, and laid Him in a manger, because there was no room for them in the inn.

Now there were in the same country shepherds living out in the fields, keeping watch over their flock by night. And behold, an Angel of The Lord stood before them, and the Glory of The Lord shone around them, and they were greatly afraid. Then the angel said to them, "Do not be afraid, for behold, I bring you good tidings of great joy which will be to all people. For there is born to you this day in the city of David a Savior, who is Christ The Lord. And this will be the sign to you: You will find a Babe wrapped in swaddling cloths, lying in a manger."

And suddenly there was with the angel a multitude of the heavenly host praising God and saying:

"Glory to God in the highest,

And on earth peace, goodwill toward men!"

So it was, when the angels had gone away from them into heaven that the shepherds said to one another, "Let us now go to Bethlehem and see this thing that has come to pass, which The Lord has made known to us." And they came with haste and found Mary and Joseph, and the Babe lying in a manger. Now when they had seen Him, they made widely known the saying which was told them concerning this Child. And all those who heard it marveled at those things which were told them by the shepherds. But Mary kept all these things and pondered them in her heart.

Luke 2:6-19

What an extraordinary moment it was for Mary to see the Savior of the World being born from her womb. The Glory of God filled that place. The angels of heaven manifested and the firmament itself surrendered to The Messiah and lit the star of heaven to announce: *this is our redeemer.* But her humble heart persevered in humility so all honor and glory would always be for the Son of God and not for herself.

Raising the Son of God must not have been an easy task, but The Father never gave Joseph and Mary that responsibility. As loving and God-fearing parents they took care of Him and educated Him. The Father, however, was the one doing the work in Jesus. No human being could have given The Messiah of the world the necessary spiritual direction.

From the time Jesus was a young boy, He expressed that He came to the world to do the works of His Father - to reconcile the world to Himself. He made this very clear even in the time when he was a child. Let's see Mary's reaction to Jesus when she found Him after three days of being missing.

"And when He was twelve years old, they went up to Jerusalem according to the custom of the feast. When they had finished the days, as they returned, the Boy Jesus lingered behind in Jerusalem. And Joseph and His mother didn't know it; but supposing Him to have been in the company, they went a day's journey, and sought Him among their relatives and acquaintances. So when they didn't find Him, they returned to Jerusalem, seeking Him. Now so it was that after three days they found Him in the temple, sitting in the midst of the teachers, both listening to them and asking them questions. And all who heard Him were astonished at His understanding and answers. So when they saw Him, they were amazed; and His mother said to Him, "Son, why have You done this to us? Look, Your father and I have sought You anxiously."

And He said to them, "Why did you seek Me? Did you not know that I must be about My Father's business?" But they didn't understand the statement which He spoke to them.

Then He went down with them and came to Nazareth, and was subject to them, but His mother kept all these things in her heart. And Jesus increased in wisdom and stature, and in favor with God and men.

Luke 2:42-52

Mary knew her Son was not like other children. She listened to Him. She didn't correct His words or scold Him for saying or doing things she didn't understand. Mary never placed herself between The Father and Jesus. This is fundamental in order to understand the heart of the *real* Mary, the mother of Our Lord. Her humble and wise character led her to be quiet and to ponder these things in her heart.

Jesus' First Miracle

In this next passage, when Jesus performs His first miracle, we see Mary's true character again. Her message is that Jesus is Lord and we are to look to Him and Him alone.

> *"On the third day there was a wedding in Cana of Galilee, and the mother of Jesus was there. Now both Jesus and His disciples were invited to the wedding. And when they ran out of wine, the mother of Jesus said to Him, "They have no wine."*
>
> *Jesus said to her, 'Woman, what does your concern have to do with Me? My hour has not yet come.'*
>
> *His mother said to the servants, 'Whatever He says to you, do it.'"*
>
> *John 2:1-5*

Time and again we see that Mary, being the mother of Jesus, was neither the ruling voice, nor the one who had the last word. It wasn't in Mary's character to impose something, or do something of her own will. She didn't say, "I beg you to perform a miracle because they don't have any more wine." She didn't impose herself like someone who had all authority and say, "You have to make wine." She always conducted herself as a faithful servant of God. She simply let Jesus know *what the need was*. This shows us that she knew Jesus had the authority to do what was needed. What good is it to present a need to someone who doesn't have the authority to solve the problem?

After this, Mary expresses what would be the most important message she would leave us: *"Whatever He says to you, do it."* In other words, she was telling those who were serving at the wedding, **"Don't come looking for me to solve your problem. He is the one who has the answers and He will tell you what you need to do."**

Mary among the Disciples

It was very important for the work of Jesus the Messiah to be the focus, which is why He protected His mother from the obvious exaltation people may be prone to give her. He loved her and He always honored her since that was a commandment of the law of His Father. That is why He referred to her as *woman*.

Jesus came to the world to save us from sin, sickness and death. It was imperative that the disciples' focus be on the work He came to do.

We see this same protection when Mary and Jesus' brothers were asking for Him.

Then His brothers and His mother came, and standing outside they sent to Him, calling Him. And a multitude was sitting around Him; and they said to Him, "Look, Your mother and Your brothers are outside seeking You."

But He answered them, saying, "Who is My mother, or My brothers?" And He looked around in a circle at those who sat about Him, and said, "Here are My mother and My brothers! For whoever does the will of God is My brother and My sister and mother."

Mark 3:31-35

Notice in this passage that Mary's attitude was not overbearing towards Jesus. She didn't enter that place like someone who had all authority, but she actually sent for Him. She didn't get offended at Jesus' response. To her, it was very clear that He is The supreme authority and He came to establish The Kingdom of God on Earth. He also came to give His family back to The Father. But who is His family? His family consists of all those who do His will, including her.

With the words Jesus used, He made it very clear that although Mary was the most blessed among women and was His own mother, she didn't have a hierarchical authority over others. He also wanted to make very clear that she was not a middle person between men and Him or The Father. He wasn't despising or scorning her, by using these words; He was protecting her from the idolatry of man.

Let's look at the hierarchy of the Kingdom of God in the passage announced by Paul the Apostle in the epistle to the Ephesians; to all those called to be saints, that is, to those who are sanctified by the Grace and Blood of Jesus:

...that the God of our Lord Jesus Christ, the Father of glory, may give to you the spirit of wisdom and revelation in the knowledge of Him, the eyes of your understanding being enlightened; that you may know what is the hope of His calling, what are the riches of the glory of His inheritance in the saints, and what is the exceeding greatness of His power toward us who believe, according to the working of His mighty power which He worked in Christ when He raised Him from the dead and seated Him at His right hand in the heavenly places, far above all principality and power and might and dominion,

and every name that is named, not only in this age but also in that which is to come. And He put all things under His feet, and gave Him to be head over all things to the church, which is His body, the fullness of Him who fills all in all.

Ephesians 1:17-23

God established His Kingdom and placed Jesus Christ as the head of all things and established a mystical body — including Mary, composed of true believers throughout the ages. She knew these principles and kept His commandments since she was at the feet of Jesus many times listening to His teachings. She knew Jesus would send The Holy Spirit to help, sustain and teach them all things. She knew she would never take the place of The Holy Spirit, which is God Himself.

But the Comforter (Counselor, Helper, Intercessor, Advocate, Strengthener, Standby), the Holy Spirit, Whom the Father will send in My name [in My place, to represent Me and act on My behalf], He will teach you all things. And He will cause you to recall (will remind you of, bring to your remembrance) everything I have told you.

John 14:26 AMP

But when the Comforter (Counselor, Helper, Advocate, Intercessor, Strengthener, Standby) comes, Whom I will send to you from the Father, the Spirit of Truth Who comes (proceeds) from the Father, He [Himself] will testify regarding Me.

John 15:26 AMP

However, I am telling you nothing but the truth when I say it is profitable (good, expedient, advantageous) for you that I go away. Because if I do not go away, the Comforter (Counselor, Helper, Advocate, Intercessor, Strengthener, Standby) will not come to you [into close fellowship with you]; but if I go away, I will send Him to you [to be in close fellowship with you].

John 16:7 AMP

Mary was present when Jesus ascended into heaven and was part of the 120 in the Upper Room who received The Holy Spirit on the day of Pentecost. She rejoiced because the Comforter had been manifested so all generations could know Him and enjoy His Love, comfort and power. The disciples that day didn't pray to Mary so the promise of the Holy Spirit would come, they prayed all together.

*And when they had entered, they went up into the upper room where they were staying: Peter, James, John, and Andrew; Philip and Thomas; Bartholomew and Matthew; James the son of Alphaeus and Simon the Zealot; and Judas the son of James. These all continued with one accord in prayer and supplication, with the women and **Mary the mother of Jesus**, and with His brothers.*

Acts 1:13-14

The God of Mary

Mary heard in the synagogue and surely knew from her own experience about the Love of The Heavenly Father and how He is our greatest comforter. Her heart rejoiced in knowing that the *Comforter* would finally come to all those who would receive Him.

Listen to Me, you who follow after righteousness, You who seek the Lord: Look to the rock from which you were hewn, And to the hole of the pit from which you were dug.

Look to Abraham your father, And to Sarah who bore you; For I called him alone, And blessed him and increased him."

For the Lord will comfort Zion, **He will comfort** *all her waste places; He will make her wilderness like Eden,*

And her desert like the garden of the Lord; Joy and gladness will be found in it, Thanksgiving and the voice of melody.

Isaiah 51:1-3

I, even **I, am He who comforts you.** *Who are you that you should be afraid of a man who will die, And of the son of a man who will be made like grass?*

Isaiah 51:12

Jesus takes care of Mary

Now there stood by the cross of Jesus His mother, and His mother's sister, Mary the wife of Clopas, and Mary Magdalene.

When Jesus therefore saw His mother, and the disciple whom He loved standing by, He said to His mother, "Woman, behold your son!" Then He said to the disciple, "Behold your mother!" And from that hour that disciple took her to his own home.

John 19:25-27

Once again in this passage we see Jesus referring to Mary as *woman* and not as mother. Aside from the protection that we already discussed, this is also due to the proper establishment of God's designs on earth. Everything Jesus did was already prophesied by the Old Testament prophets.

Surely the Lord God does nothing,
Unless He reveals His secret to His servants the prophets.

Amos 3:7

According to the Old Testament prophecies, a divine order was established. This order recognizes one God, in the persons of The Father, The Son and The Holy Spirit. Nowhere had the Lord established a *"Mother of Humanity"*. The Kingdom of God revolves around The Father. If God would have wanted a mother for His children, he would have spoken about her, and Mary and Jesus would have made the world know that she had come.

Jesus always expressed that He came to earth to reveal His Father, who is sufficient to fulfill all of man's spiritual, emotional and physical needs.

Jesus said to him, "Have I been with you so long, and yet you have not known Me, Philip? He who has seen Me has seen the Father; so how can you say, Show us the Father?"

John 14:9

All things have been delivered to Me by My Father, and no one knows who the Son is except the Father, and who the Father is except the Son, and the one to whom the Son wills to reveal Him.

Luke 10:22

Jesus loved his earthly mother by placing her in John, the Beloved's hands, but He was not establishing Her as mother over Earth. If that were the case, it would have been prophesied in the Old Testament.

In our next chapter we will find out where this theory to worship a mother goddess comes from and when it did start. Also it will become clear how this spirit opposes The Father, The Son and even Mary herself.

CHAPTER 4

THE REAL MARY
VERSUS
THE FALSE MARY

Up to this point we've been analyzing aspects of the personality, character and beliefs of the *real* Mary. We will now take an in-depth look at the *false* Mary.

I mentioned earlier that God had already prepared His plan of salvation from the very moment man fell in the Garden of Eden. He announced it while cursing the serpent. The Son of God, the seed of Mary, would crush the serpent's head and the serpent would bruise His heel. This was a reference to His death on the cross where satan would be destroyed and Jesus would be raised from the dead.

> *And I will put enmity between you and the woman, and between your seed and her Seed; He shall crush your head, and you shall bruise His heel.*
>
> *Genesis 3:15*

An enormous hatred towards women was established in the devil from that moment. From generation to generation, women have been denigrated and abused in multiple ways, but the devil's focus was on the woman from which his lethal opponent would be born.

The devil's plan thousands of years before Christ

The devil devised a plan he hoped would cause major damage to God while using the woman figure. He would disguise himself as a queen, a goddess so wonderful, that the eyes of the world would be directed to her. That way he could rob the worship from God. He knew perfectly well that this is what caused his fall, as it's the greatest offense anyone can do to God.

> *How you are fallen from heaven, O Lucifer, son of the morning!*
> *How you are cut down to the ground, You who weakened the nations!*
>
> *For you have said in your heart: 'I will ascend into heaven,*
> *I will exalt my throne above the stars of God; I will also sit on the mount of the congregation on the farthest sides of the north;* **I will ascend above the heights of the clouds, I will be like the Most High.**

> *Isaiah 14:12-14*

Although God rejected him, satan's wicked heart persisted to dwell on this plan. He wanted to sit on the throne above in the heavens and be like God. He had been the heavenly worship leader and now desired that worship for himself. As a result, he carried out his evil plan and disguised himself as a character that would be easily accepted. He called it "The Queen of Heaven".

Since heaven is established around The Father, the devil himself established his realm around a "queen mother".

What we will now discover in the following research is that this queen has absolutely nothing to do with Mary, the mother of Our Lord. This "Queen of Heaven" was created and worshipped thousands of years before Christ.

Origin of the Queen of Heaven

It all started at the dawn of civilization, in the Paleolithic age. satan inspired humanity to create sculptures of feminine images and to worship them. Figurines that have been discovered by archeologists clearly show an exaltation of fertility. Man, who eats of the fruit of the earth begins to worship the earth as a mother and in exchange for the benefits obtained from her, he makes clay or stone renderings to offer up to her as worship.

Among the most ancient we find, "Venus of Laussel" and "Venus of Lespugue."[4] In these grotesque figurines we can clearly see the exaltation of maternity as a symbol of mother earth.

Fig. 4 — Venus of Laussel

---

[4] *Investigation by Apostle Fernando Orihuela*

Fig. 5 — Venus of Lespugue

The worship of woman as the transmitter of life developed a "matriarchal system" among the first civilizations. The most prominent of them was Babylon, the first great city on earth where this worship developed into a much more organized religious and governmental system.

Babylon

Babylon is the mother of all civilizations on earth. The Bible tells the foundation of this great city and how it became the cultural hub out of which all idolatrous worship came from on earth.

Now the whole earth had one language and one speech. And it came to pass, as they journeyed from the east, that they found a plain in the land of Shinar, and they dwelt there. Then they said to one another, "Come, let us make bricks and bake them thoroughly." They had brick for stone, and they had asphalt for mortar. And they said, "Come, let us build ourselves a city, and a tower whose top is in the heavens; let us make a name for ourselves, lest we be scattered abroad over the face of the whole earth."

But the Lord came down to see the city and the tower which the sons of men had built. And the Lord said, "Indeed the people are one and they all have one language, and this is what they begin to do; now nothing that they propose to do will be withheld from them. Come, let us go down and there confuse their language, that they may not understand one another's speech." So the Lord scattered them abroad from there over the face of all the earth, and they ceased building the city.

Genesis 11:1-8

Babylon was built in Mesopotamia by a man named Nimrod who was the first powerful person on earth (*Genesis 10:8*). He was a bloodthirsty man who also established other great cities in the ancient world, such as Nineveh. Babylon was considered one of the Seven Wonders of the Ancient World due to its hanging gardens and the famous Tower of Babel.

The word Babel, which became the city's name, means "confusion". Not only because the languages of the nations were confused, but also because satan would use the system he established there to confuse and blind the understanding of the later nations. In a spiritual sense, it's a place of government, and the strategy behind it was to mix the pagan and the sacred to deceive humanity and fulfill the enemy's evil objectives.

Fig. 6 — Tower of Babel

Fig. 7 — Hanging Gardens of Babylon

Legends and oral traditions passed down generations from those who lived during that time state that Nimrod, the founder of Babylon, was married to Queen Semiramis. He proclaimed himself as "the god of the sun" and she established herself as "the goddess of fertility and sexuality, the goddess of the moon and the night."

satan, in order to govern the world grabbed hold of this couple and taught them all kind of witchcraft in an attempt to unite the universe and Earth together. He needed to establish his rulers in the constellations as well as in the nations. Let's keep in mind that when Lucifer fell he brought with him one-third of the stars, which are fallen angels.

> *And another sign appeared in heaven: behold, a great, fiery red dragon having seven heads and ten horns, and seven diadems on his heads. His tail drew a third of the stars of heaven and threw them to the earth.*
>
> *Revelation 12:3-4a*

This is why we will always see a constant interaction with the stars of the sky in his government. All Babylonian symbolism is loaded with sun, moon and star figures.

Now satan not only needed to establish and impose a celestial hierarchy of *his* gods, but he needed to steal the concept of the virgin and child that was announced since the fall of man. From generation to generation, Adam and Eve's descendants passed on the hope of a future Savior. The devil used this ideology and distorted it in order to obtain the acceptance and credibility from his deceived followers.

Sometime after Nimrod's death, Semiramis became pregnant and gave birth to Tammuz. Semiramis took advantage of the anticipated prophecy of the Messiah and to cover her sin, proclaimed herself as the virgin who gave birth to the promised son. The queen argued that Nimrod himself, the god of the sun had reincarnated in Tammuz, who was conceived in a supernatural way. From that moment on the worship of mother and child began, and expanded to all civilizations. As a matter of fact, during the Gulf War in 1991, a bomb's explosion led to the discovery of clay tablets containing that early days' prophecy. Babylon was founded precisely in the area that is now modern day Iraq.

When God confused the languages at the Tower of Babel, the people dispersed and established themselves all over Mesopotamia, central Asia and various parts of Europe. Every one of these civilizations took with them the worship of mother and child as a religious model. The mother goddess took on different names and forms of worship according to the different languages and cultures.

Queen of Heaven in Diverse Civilizations

Once the people were dispersed throughout the world, there was an evolution of Semiramis as she was transformed into various goddesses. The first one that emerged was "Inanna," the Queen of Heaven among the Sumerians, goddess of love, fertility and war. After this came "Ishtar", who took Semiramis' place among the Mesopotamians, as the goddess of war and lady of battles. There was also "Astarte, Asera or Ashtoreth" among the Canaanites.[5]

These three are the oldest representations of the mother goddess.

---

[5] *Study regarding the Queen of Heaven by Apostle Fernando Orihuela.*

We'll now look at how they are repeated along with their symbolism in many civilizations even today. "Isis" was among the Egyptians, "Pachamama" among the Incas, "Tonatzin" among the Aztecs, "Venus" among the Romans, "Durga" among the Hindus, "Diana" among the Greeks and many more.

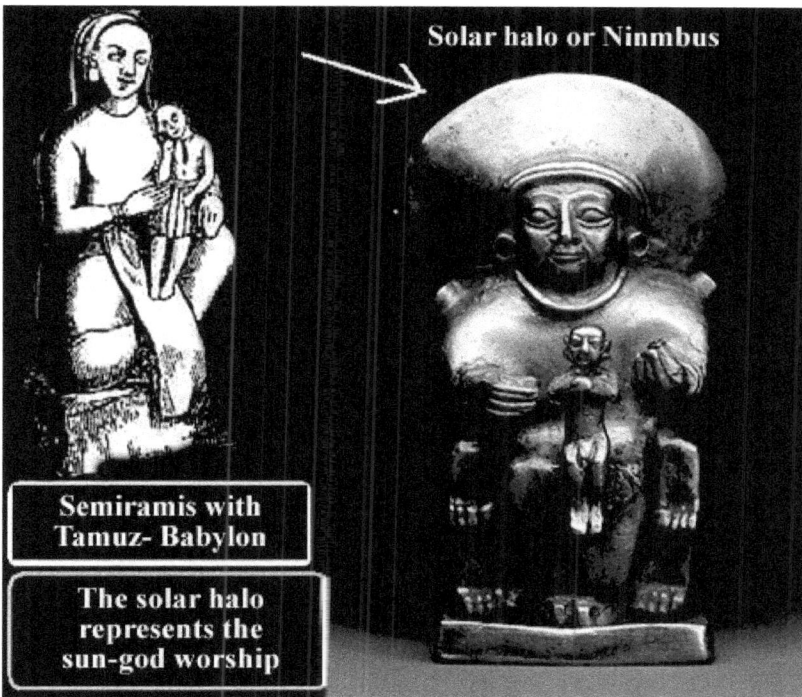

Solar halo or Ninmbus

Semiramis with Tamuz- Babylon

The solar halo represents the sun-god worship

Fig. 8 — Semiramis with Tamuz

*Fig. 9 — Isis Lactans Pio Clementine Museum
Egyptian Goddess Isis with child*

Fig. 10 — Egyptian Isis - The Solar Disc of Osiris over her

Fig. 11 — Pachamama, Inca Goddess, Mother of the Earth

Fig. 12 — Hindu Goddess with child and a lion

In this next figure we see "Inanna" with her various symbols, such as water that brings rain, the half-moon (on her head in this case), the lion and the eight-pointed star (wheels of the car)

Fig. 13 — Goddess Inanna

Fig. 14 — European Inanna

Here (Fig. 14) we see the same Inanna in a European version. In this Dutch painting we see a representation of the Queen of Heaven surrounded by lions edifying a temple for her to be worshipped.

As you look through the various portrayals of Ishtar, notice the sharing of these symbols in Mesopotamia. The lion is one of her main guardians at the door of the temple of Ishtar. The temple was originally built in Babylon and was transferred to the Museum of Pergamon in Berlin.

Fig. 15 — Ishtar atop lions

Fig. 16 — Fragment, Lions at the Ishtar-Gate[6]

*Fig. 17 — Ishtar shown as the goddess Isis in Egypt,
with a lion close to her.*

---

[6] *Pergamon Museum, Berlin, Germany*

Fig. 18 — Durga, Hindus mother goddess, the solar disc, the arc, the fleur de lys, are all symbols of Inanna.

Another one of Ishtar's main symbols is the eight-pointed star. We see this symbol in many representations of this particular goddess in the different expressions in which she has been identified, as well as the fleur de lys.

Fig. 19 — Goddess Cybele with lions

Fig. 20 — Ishtar with a lion, a star, a bow in her head and arrows

Fig. 21 — Young girl being consecrated to Ishtar before a priest

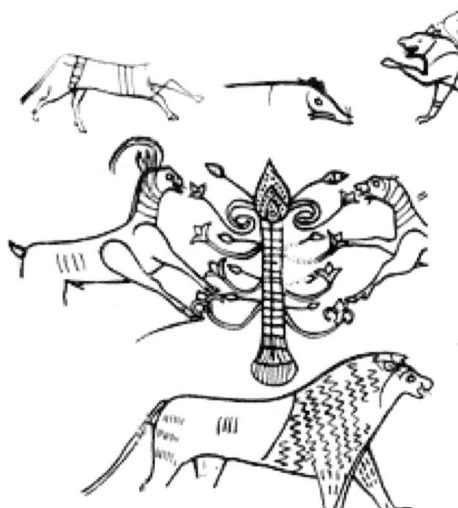

Fig. 22 — Fleur de lys and Ishtar's animal guardians

Fig. 23 — Ishtar in the pre-Columbian age in the form of the Aztec goddess Tonatzin.

We see the eight-pointed star formed by triangles and the fleur de lys. The rose is another one of the symbols we will see repeated in these deities of fertility and love. The most ancient rose is found in the Egyptian goddess, Isis. From there we will see it repeat itself in many other goddesses such as Venus, Artemis and Aphrodite.

Fig. 24 — Isis receiving roses

Fig. 25 — Artemis at the Toledo cathedral crowned with roses

This pagan worship with its great diversity is what the prophets of the Old Testament had to face. Time and again we see in Israel's history how the people would deviate from God and would unavoidably fall into goddess' worship.

> *They forsook the Lord and served Baal and the Ashtoreths.*
>
> *Judges 2:13*

Worshipping goddesses placed a veil over the people's understanding so they wouldn't realize how much they were offending God. This goddess, the Queen of Heaven, is in no way, Mary the mother of Our Lord. It's a deceiving spirit that existed many centuries before Christ was born. She has the kind of power that haunts people's souls throughout generations, and when she feels threatened, she stirs up people with such anger that they close their hearts and become deaf to what God is saying.

God is good and merciful and wants the best for us, but if there is one thing that is an abomination to Him it's idolatry. He condemns it with great anger.

In the *Book of Jeremiah*, written between 628 B.C. and 580 B.C., we clearly see the Queen of Heaven tormenting the hearts of the people of Israel as she does today.

> *Now therefore, thus says the Lord, the God of hosts, the God of Israel: 'Why do you commit this great evil against yourselves, to cut off from you man and woman, child and infant, out of Judah, leaving none to remain, in that you provoke Me to wrath with the works of your*

hands, burning incense to other gods in the land of Egypt where you have gone to dwell, that you may cut yourselves off and be a curse and a reproach among all the nations of the earth?

Jeremiah 44:7-8

Then all the men who knew that their wives had burned incense to other gods, with all the women who stood by, a great multitude, and all the people who dwelt in the land of Egypt, in Pathros, answered Jeremiah, saying: "As for the word that you have spoken to us in the name of the Lord, we will not listen to you! But we will certainly do whatever has gone out of our own mouth, to burn incense to the queen of heaven and pour out drink offerings to her, as we have done, we and our fathers, our kings and our princes, in the cities of Judah and in the streets of Jerusalem. For then we had plenty of food, were well-off, and saw no trouble.

Jeremiah 44:15-17

Notice the women's harsh reaction, blinded by the spiritual dominance of the Queen of Heaven. **"We will not listen to the word that comes from Jehovah."** This spirit is real and operates in millions of people now, separating them from the will of God and blinding their understanding. God becomes furious with this. Look at how He responded to those women with great indignation in this next verse.

Behold, I will watch over them for adversity and not for good. And all the men of Judah who are in the land of Egypt shall be consumed by the sword and by famine, until there is an end to them. Yet a small number who escape the sword shall return from the land of Egypt to the land of Judah; and all the remnant of Judah, who have gone to the land of Egypt to dwell there, shall know whose words will stand; Mine or theirs.

Jeremiah 44:27-28

As we saw at the beginning of the scriptures in Jeremiah, worship to the Queen of Heaven brings great harm to her followers. Many people suffer with misery, theft, sickness, deep pain and misfortune.

Why do you commit this great evil against yourselves ...

This is reflected during the time of Judges when Israel was a victim of terrible famines and theft when the Midianites continuously took everything they had. This was because they worshipped the goddess, Asera[7] or Astarte, Queen of Heaven among the Canaanites.

God manifests in Gideon and raises him as a deliverer. God tells Gideon it's necessary for him to demolish the altar his father erected for the goddess Asera, so that God may deliver them from famine and persecution of the Midianites.

Now it came to pass the same night that the Lord said to him, "Take your father's young bull, the second bull of seven years old, and tear down the altar of Baal that your father has, and cut down the wooden image that is beside it; and build an altar to the Lord your God on top of this

---

[7] *Asera is a representation similar to Astarte or Ashtoreth.*

rock in the proper arrangement, and take the second bull and offer a burnt sacrifice with the wood of the image which you shall cut down.

Judges 6:25-26

Let's look at Babylon again for a moment, with satan's plan to govern the earth and separate man from the true God. Not only did satan desires to be worshipped, but he also had to raise up a kingdom where he would subdue all nations. As I've mentioned, his strategy was to create the deceiving character referred to as "Queen of Heaven."

Not only was Babylon a city that existed in ancient times, but it's also a spiritual city that continues to reign over all nations today. Babylon represents an entire spiritual authoritative system blocking the hearts of mankind from seeing and hearing the truth. In the Book of Revelation, Babylon is represented as a great harlot.

The woman was arrayed in purple and scarlet, and adorned with gold and precious stones and pearls, having in her hand a golden cup full of abominations and the filthiness of her fornication. And on her forehead a name was written: MYSTERY, BABYLON THE GREAT, THE MOTHER OF HARLOTS AND OF THE ABOMINATIONS OF THE EARTH. I saw the woman, drunk with the blood of the saints and with the blood of the martyrs of Jesus. And when I saw her, I marveled with great amazement.

Revelation 17:4-6 Emphasis by the author

And the woman whom you saw is that great city which reigns over the kings of the earth."

Revelation 17:18

It's clear Babylon is a spiritual government and the Queen of Heaven is seated on that very throne.

Fig. 26 — Statue of the great harlot located at Lake Constance in Konstanz, Germany holding a king and a pope in her hands.

Creation of the False Mary

I mentioned how satan developed a strong enmity or hostility towards Mary because she was the one God designated to carry and give birth to the Messiah. As a result, satan devised a plan in his disturbed and wicked mind that would not only hurt the Father's heart, but the Son's and Mary's heart as well. That is when he decided to create the "*false*" Mary.

For thousands of years he established and developed a strategy to direct mankind's worship away from God and towards the Queen of Heaven. Then the apex of his plan was to steal the name of the mother of Our Lord and mix it with the name of his abominable creation.

The devil's great opportunity came when John the Apostle took Mary, the mother of Jesus, to live with him in the city of Ephesus. John took her as his own mother when Jesus announced it from the cross. John and Mary lived for years in that city in Asia Minor.

Ephesus was known for its worship of Diana. This deity garnered great profits for all craftsman who created idols in her likeness. Asia and the entire world at that time were captive under Diana's worship. When Paul the Apostle went to Ephesus to evangelize he found himself in a great spiritual battle with this power of darkness.

For a certain man named Demetrius, a silversmith, who made silver shrines of Diana, brought no small profit to the craftsmen. He called them together with the workers of similar occupation, and said: "Men, you know that we have our prosperity by this trade. Moreover you see and hear that not only at Ephesus, but throughout almost all Asia, this Paul has persuaded and turned away many people, saying that they are not gods which are made with hands. So not only is this trade of ours in danger of falling into disrepute, but also the temple of the great goddess Diana may be despised and her magnificence destroyed, whom all Asia and the world worship." Now when they heard this, they were full of wrath and cried out, saying, "Great is Diana of the Ephesians!"

Acts 19:24-28

Ephesus was the place where the Queen of Heaven most manifested in the time of the apostles. Ephesus also happened to be the home of Mary, the woman satan targeted.

The devil waited patiently for John, the last of the apostles, to die because had John been alive, he would never have allowed satan's plan to mix Mary with Diana of Ephesus to take place.

This goddess was considered the "mother of humanity" and for this reason her image consisted of a woman with many breasts for nursing the entire world.

Upon Mary's death, God strategically caused her body to disappear just like He did with Moses' body. Had their bodies fallen into the hands of man they would have been torn up by idolaters.

> *Yet Michael the archangel, in contending with the devil, when he disputed about the body of Moses, dared not bring against him a reviling accusation, but said, "The Lord rebuke you!"*
>
> *Jude 1:9*

Historically, an empty tomb exists which was dedicated to Mary. Some of the apocryphal books state that after her death she was taken to heaven by angels. To be taken bodily into the realm of eternity is a verifiable act in the Bible. It happened to two prophets of the Old Testament - Enoch and Elijah.[8]

---

[8] *"And Enoch walked with God; and he was not, for God took him." Genesis 5:24*

"Then it happened, as they continued on and talked, that suddenly a chariot of fire appeared with horses of fire, and separated the two of them; and Elijah went up by a whirlwind into heaven." 2 Kings 2:11

The truth is, just like Moses' body, her body was not left in a well-known place.

It was only in 1958 when Mary's assumption was accepted by the Vatican. After centuries without biblical verdict it's difficult and practically impossible to know what really happened to Mary's body.

More than 200 years after John the Apostle's death, Constantine, the Roman Emperor, had a vision of a cross and a voice saying, "You will triumph under this symbol."

From that moment on the emperor declared himself a Christian and he stopped the persecution of his brothers in the faith and promoted the Roman Empire's new religion. However, since he had little revelation and no counsel from the fathers of the Church, he decided to mix pagan gods with eminent figures of Christianity. This act helped him unite his empire as it was beginning to fall apart.

This is how the devil accomplished his perfect plan to usurp Mary's name and mix it with pagan worship. This *false* Mary took the place of Diana of the Ephesians, of Venus among the Romans and she became the new "Queen of Heaven." In the year 431 A.D. at the Council of Ephesus, Mary was proclaimed "mother of God" and "Queen of Heaven." Her first image is made and configured in the same position as Diana of Ephesus.

Fig. 27 — Diana of Ephesus

Fig. 28 — The False Mary (Virgin of Ephesus)

*Fig. 29 — Diana of Ephesus being crowned by angels
as Queen of Heaven.*

Notice the lion, symbol of Inanna and Ishtar on the pedestal. The
figurines of nude angels and those surrounding her are clear
symbols of fertility goddesses.

Fig. 30 — Altarpiece of the false *Mary*

Look at the similarities between this altarpiece of the *false* Mary being crowned in the same manner by nude angels above the moon of Inanna.

The Real Mary, the Mother of Jesus

Mary, the holy mother of Jesus, God fearing, despiser of all idolatry and faithful in keeping all the commandments The Father and Jesus established must have felt and continues to feel great sorrow.

The *real* Mary would never have allowed something like this. She never positioned herself above the Church. She never proclaimed herself as a mediator between God and man. She knew that place only belonged to Jesus.

> *For there is one God and one Mediator between God and men, the Man Christ Jesus*
>
> 1 Timothy 2:5

Jesus crushed the head of the serpent, and the serpent bruised His heel by making His mother an idol.

It's very important to understand that Mary, the mother of Jesus and Mary, the Queen of Heaven or *false* Mary, are two completely different spirits, with different intentions.

The *real* Mary, who knows and honors God, leads us to worship Him and only Him. Mary would never seek worship because she understood her Son's mission here on earth. Jesus was the one and only sufficient Savior who died for our sins, took our infirmities and defeated death to give us eternal life. Mary could never have accomplished this and it was never her mission to do so.

Her message was clear and is summarized in one phrase,

"Whatever He says to you, do it." *(John 2:5)*

Mary knew The Eternal Father and all her worship was dedicated to Him. She fulfilled all His commandments written in the Law of Moses, in the Psalms and in the Prophets. She would never have allowed sculptures to be crafted with the purpose of worshipping her.

I am the Lord, that is My name; And My glory I will not give to another, Nor My praise to carved images.

Isaiah 42:8

God detests Babylon, its idols, its Queen of Heaven and all of its demonic symbols. He wants to cleanse all those who genuinely seek Him and have been deceived by this lie from hell.

It's necessary to understand these things and to be able to differentiate between the *real* Mary and the *false* Mary. God is judging Babylon and its queen. Undoubtedly, it will fall along with everything else that is false.

Come down and sit in the dust, O virgin daughter of Babylon;

Sit on the ground without a throne, O daughter of the Chaldeans! For you shall no more be called Tender and delicate.

Isaiah 47:1

Sit in silence, and go into darkness, O daughter of the Chaldeans; For you shall no longer be called The Lady of Kingdoms.

Isaiah 47:5

81

Mary is the mother of Our Lord and the most blessed among women. The Bible says to give honor where honor is due. To honor is to recognize someone for who they are and for their works, but it does not mean we should worship or bow down before them. This should only be done before God.

The *real* Mary is in heaven in a very special place around the throne of God, but she is not God nor does she have the attributes of The Almighty. She is not omnipresent. She is not able to be everywhere listening to billions of people. She knows that only Jesus Christ can do this because He is God, our high priest and intercessor.

Also there were many priests, because they were prevented by death from continuing. But He, because He continues forever, has an unchangeable priesthood. Therefore He is also able to save to the uttermost those who come to God through Him, since He always lives to make intercession for them.

For such a High Priest was fitting for us, who is holy, harmless, undefiled, separate from sinners, and has become higher than the heavens;

Hebrews 7:23-26

When John, the Apostle was taken up to heaven where the Book of Revelation was given to him, he fell at the feet of the angel who was revealing all of these things, but the angel rebuked him for doing so.

Then he said to me, "Write: 'Blessed are those who are called to the marriage supper of the Lamb!'" And he said to me, "These are the true sayings of God." And I fell at his feet to worship him. But he said to me, "See that you do not do that! I am your fellow servant, and of your brethren who have the testimony of Jesus. Worship God! For the testimony of Jesus is the spirit of prophecy."

Revelation 19:9,10

If Mary could speak to us today she would say, "Do not bow before me. Worship God. I am a fellow servant of all the brethren who have the testimony of Jesus."

We will later discuss the correct position - according to the Word of God - that we should take before Mary.

CHAPTER 5

THE QUEEN OF HEAVEN
OR FALSE MARY
AFTER THE 4TH CENTURY, A.D.

Now that we've studied the characteristics and main symbols of the Queen of Heaven through Semiramis, Inanna, Ishtar and Ashtoreth, let's see how these symbols and characteristics are reflected on all of the iconography (the art and images) that were made for the *false* Mary, as well as her temples after the fourth century.

Fig. 31 — Lions door at the Cathedral in Toledo. Here we can identify Ishtar's symbols: The lions, the solar disc and the fleur de lys.

When the name of the *false* Mary mixed with goddesses of all cultures and the diverse attributes and powers, an infinite number of different images surged. She adapted to different races and adopted many names. She would not only be falsely called Mary, but in many cases she took on names and attributes of goddesses that came before Christ. Some images would be more miraculous than others.

The Cubans would say that "La Caridad del Cobre" (Our Lady of Charity) is more powerful than other images. Mexicans will not worship the black Madonna of Poland, but will worship the Virgin of Guadalupe. The French worship that of Lourdes, but they will not follow the Virgin of Fatima, who reigns over Portugal.

Some may say that the Virgin of Conception is more powerful than the Virgin of Carmen and some may say the opposite. As a matter of fact, it's estimated there are 2,850 different virgin names. Some virgins are black, some are white, some are modest, some are triumphant, some are ostentatious and some are sorrowful.

Fig. 32 / Fig. 8 — Black Virgin of Montserrat Spain in the same position as Semiramis with Tamuz (from page 59)

Fig. 33 — Virgen de Guadalupe,
in the same position as Tonatzin, the Aztec goddess

Fig. 34 — Black Madonna with Solar Circle and fleur de lyz,
round beads necklace and pendant. We also see in this picture the
symbols of the Hindu goddess Durga,

Fig. 35 — Goddess Durga, solar circle, fleur de lyz,
round beads necklace and pendant

Fig. 36 — Venus with roses and naked angels

*Fig. 37 — Madonna with naked angels, roses
and the moon of Ishtar*

Fig. 38 — Ishtar usurping Mary's image.

(Fig. 38 on previous page) Notice how she is the one receiving the crown of the kingdom, the Father and Jesus don't have crowns. Jesus has the eight-point star, symbol of Isthar on his clothes and Mary has the fleur de lys and the eight-point star upon her head.

Remember that satan's plan is to place himself above God so he is the one that appears to be crowned and reigning above The Father and Jesus, stripping them of their Glory. For this very reason whenever we see most images of the Queen of Heaven or *false* Mary with Jesus and The Father, we see she is crowned and they are not.

Fig. 39 — Star, Isthar's Sun and Moon

Here we have Ishtar and Inanna's symbols; the 8-point star, the moon and the sun. In the following image we can see them surrounding the false Mary.

*Fig. 40 — In this image we can also see how she has the crown
and The Father and Son are bowing before her.*

There are temples dedicated and built for the *false* Mary where
you can clearly see that she is the Queen of Heaven and there is
no room for anyone else. She occupies the main altar and you
don't see Jesus resurrected or reigning, but He is dead on a small
cross or as a baby in her arms. As long as the heir to a throne is an
infant, he has no kingdom or authority. That's exactly how the
devil wants to project Jesus. Not as the one who defeated him and
took all dominion over the earth from him.

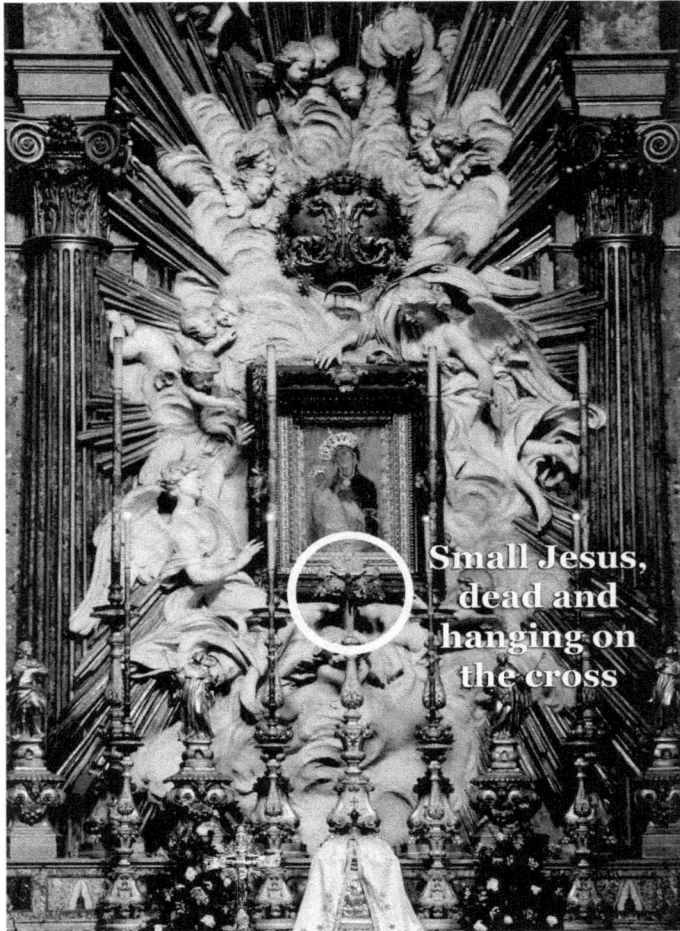

Fig. 41 — Main altar of the Queen of Heaven in the church of the Most Holy Name of Mary. Notice the contrast in the gigantic altar to the queen and the tiny figure of Jesus hanging on the cross without a kingdom or authority.

May God open our eyes and expand our understanding, so we see the light of the gospel and the darkness of the devil's tricks.

Idolatry blinds and deafens those who practice it and the price that is paid is not being able to enter the Kingdom of God.

Their idols are silver and gold, The work of men's hands.

They have mouths, but they do not speak; Eyes they have, but they do not see;

They have ears, but they do not hear; Noses they have, but they do not smell;

They have hands, but they do not handle; Feet they have, but they do not walk; Nor do they mutter through their throat.

Those who make them are like them; So is everyone who trusts in them.

Psalms 115:4-8

But the cowardly, unbelieving, abominable, murderers, sexually immoral, sorcerers, idolaters, and all liars shall have their part in the lake which burns with fire and brimstone, which is the second death.

Revelation 21:8

Idolatry should not be taken lightly. Understanding idolatry is crucial because it affects the eternal destiny of man.

CHAPTER 6

THE WAY, THE TRUTH AND THE LIFE

Despite my encounter with the Virgin of Garabandal I felt a deep void in my heart. The repetitive prayers of the rosary became monotonous and didn't satisfy my spiritual search. There had to be something more. I wanted to live a genuine life with God so I could feel Him like the great heroes of the faith, but I only had the scarce memory of my mystical experiences.

Life had dealt me severe blows. I sank deeper into pain with each passing day. I was a victim of horrible betrayals, abuses, violence, theft and affronts of all kinds. My health and finances were failing. I felt like I was in a bottomless pit. I spent nine years where my outlook on life was so depressing that I literally hit rock bottom.

My desperate prayers were like vanishing smoke without answers and without light in a long night that seemed as though it would never end.

I ended up in a hospital on the verge of suicide. I fell into a terrible depression. I was without hope until one day a young man walked into my room. He was friendly and his eyes radiated a peace I had never seen. He spoke to me about Jesus Christ, the Son of God. No one had ever spoken to me about the Love of God like he did.

As he spoke I could literally see Jesus before me nailed to the cross. I felt his gaze piercing my heart and speaking these silent words,

"I did this out of love for you and if you were the only person in all the earth, I would have still done it just for you."

The way Jesus looked at me was so real. For a moment I thought He was in the room with us.

I then heard the words spoken by my visitor as he repeated Jesus' words, *"I am the way, the truth and the life and no one comes to the Father except through me."*

A glowing light illuminated all of my being when he said that. It was the Power of Truth manifesting on the inside. Jesus Christ IS THE WAY, not a way, but the only way to reconcile us with The Father.

I wanted Jesus. I wanted the living Jesus who was instantly transforming my depression and loneliness into hope. At the same time His light was confronting me with the reality of my filthy soul, full of so many sins. "How could Jesus forgive me?" I thought, as I felt reproved by the presence of His holiness in the room. He was so pure, so holy, so perfect and I was a sinner, unworthy and shattered, with nothing to offer Him.

I began to cry, repentant and longing for His Mercy and marvelous Love. I was all pain and tears, as I saw the wickedness and ugliness of my soul. Then the hands of the young man came upon my head and with conviction he said, "Jesus, forgive all of her sins and cleanse her of all wickedness with your precious blood that you shed on the cross for her."

Something happened in that moment. A weight was lifted off me and a mantle of guilt and pain was gone. Everything left me and I felt as if I could fly.

The young man spoke again, "Now invite Jesus to live inside of you and make a covenant of salvation with Him," he said. "*The wages of sin is death, but the gift of God is eternal life.* He is going to fill you with His Life and will teach you all things."

I did just that - with all my heart I invited Jesus to live inside of me. And from that marvelous day on He lives in me. As He himself said, "*I will not leave you orphans; I will come to you.*"

He truly is The Way, The Truth and The Life and the One who fills the void inside of every man with peace.

My life radically changed that day. And just like that, Jesus can change the life of anyone who will follow Him and who will allow Him to live in their heart. The sun came out and the night that lasted for nine years finally came to an end.

I was learning how to follow Jesus and honor Him for who He really is: The King of Kings and Lord of Lords. He is no longer dead or nailed on the cross, but He is resurrected, alive and reconciling the world to His Father.

> (Jesus said,) "*And this is eternal life, that they may know You, the only true God, and Jesus Christ whom You have sent.*"
>
> *John 17:3*

CHAPTER 7

ENCOUNTER WITH
THE TRUTH

After the powerful encounter I had with Jesus Christ, I began to study the Bible with the help of *Christian*, the young man who visited me in the hospital. Christian was a Bible teacher and leader of a church group that met in a family home.

The first thing I did was read the New Testament. It came alive as I read it. It was as if God Himself was speaking to me, highlighting certain scriptures He wanted me to focus on.

During one of Christian's visits, I told him about my experience with the Virgin of Garabandal and I asked him if I could share it with the group. He smiled and said it was very interesting, but that all spiritual experiences needed to be confirmed with the Word of God. He said, "you should pray before sharing something like that publically."

I was surprised at his reply, because my experience was just unquestionable. I had never met anyone who had questioned whether an apparition of the virgin was from God or not. I appreciated Christian's advice, but I wanted an answer from The Lord. I decided to write down what I wanted to share with the other students.

As I jotted down the experience from my notes, I was getting very uncomfortable. Did I really need to pray about this? Why was I doubting something that so radically impacted my life?

But again, had it really changed my life for the better? Thousands of questions and many scriptures raced through my mind. I was after all, a new Believer and a novice in the things of The Kingdom of God.

Suddenly, fear came upon me. It was as if something very holy inside of me didn't want to do anything that could offend my beloved Heavenly Father. It was the very presence of Jesus who now lived inside of me calling my encounter into question.

I had no experience in getting an answer from God, so I naively opened the Bible on a random page and a scripture jumped out as if a magnifying glass were over it.

One thing I have desired of the Lord, That will I seek: That I may dwell in the house of the Lord All the days of my life, To behold the beauty of the Lord, And to inquire in His temple.

Psalms 27:4

I learned from my Bible studies that we've been established by God to be the holy temple where His presence abides. Jesus gave us the Holy Spirit to guide us to all truth and we could ask Him anything.

Nevertheless I tell you the truth. It is to your advantage that I go away; for if I do not go away, the Helper will not come to you; but if I depart, I will send Him to you.

John 16:7

However, when He, the Spirit of truth, has come, He will guide you into all truth; for He will not speak on His own authority, but whatever He hears He will speak; and He will tell you things to come. He will glorify Me, for He will take of what is Mine and declare it to you. All things that the Father has are Mine. Therefore I said that He will take of Mine and declare it to you.

John 16:13-15

After reading this scripture, I dared to ask The Lord the direct question: "Lord Jesus, will you please speak to me about my encounter with the Virgin of Garabandal?"

I waited quietly because I had great faith He would answer me. I then heard a soft, clear voice inside my spirit. It was definitely not my imagination.

He said, "*It's necessary to test every spirit because not all messengers of light are from The Father. What did the spirit, which you call the virgin, say to you?*"

At that moment I was in shock. First, because of the surprise I felt knowing He actually answered me, and second, because of the question itself. I remembered and analyzed everything as I relived it in my mind.

I then answered, "She told me to … pray the rosary every day."

Immediately the Lord's soft voice interrupted me on the inside, "*And what does My Word say regarding that?*"

I replied, "That we should not use vain repetitions as the heathen do."[9]

"What else did she say?" He asked.

"That she knew the day and the hour of the end times and that she would gather all her children in Garabandal." I said.

"And what did I say regarding this when I was on the earth?" He pressed further.

"That no one knew the day or the time, only The Father in Heaven." I responded.

I was taken aback because of what He said.

Then He clearly said, *"Read Galatians 1:8."*

> *But even if we, or an angel from heaven, preach any other gospel to you than what we have preached to you, let him be accursed.*
>
> *Galatians 1:8*

When I read *Galatians 1:8* my experience with "the virgin" became clear to me. Suddenly, everything I thought about my encounter was falling apart. I was speechless. Only God could have convinced me of the truth behind my supernatural experience. When someone lives through something like that no man on earth can convince them that such an experience doesn't come from God.

---

[9] *"But you, when you pray, go into your room, and when you have shut your door, pray to your Father who is in the secret place; and your Father who sees in secret will reward you openly. And when you pray, do not use vain repetitions as the heathen do. For they think that they will be heard for their many words. "Therefore do not be like them. For your Father knows the things you have need of before you ask Him." Matthew 6:6-8*

Christian had remarkable wisdom for such a young Bible teacher. As human beings we are so weak when it comes to supernatural encounters and unusual events in the invisible realm. If we don't have truth as our anchor, we are easily deceived.

Through the centuries, the Bible has been forgotten and put aside by millions of people who profess to believe in the Gospel of Jesus. The Bible is the legacy He left us to live according to the truth. What man says, even the most prominent in the faith, is still inferior to the Word of God. It's very important that we take the time to study the Bible, so we will not be deceived. Above all, because it's His Word that will judge us in the end. How can we possibly reject it or treat it as something unimportant in our lives?

> *He who rejects Me, and does not receive My words, has that which judges him — the word that I have spoken will judge him in the last day.*
>
> *John 12:48*

His Word is our inheritance, our blessing and the only peace capable of iluminating our path.

> *Your word is a lamp to my feet and a light to my path.*
>
> *Psalms 119:105*

We are living in a time when many supernatural events, apparitions and manifestations from the invisible world are taking place. They are either from God or satan, which is why we need to be sure and know that what we believe about them has an accurate basis in God and not in man's fables or false angels of light sent to deceive and divert us.

I loved Jesus when I practiced the Catholic faith I was brought up in, but I didn't have a foundation of truth which is the Word of God. I was deceived by an angel of light that diverted me from faith in Jesus Christ and centered me on what I know now to be the "*false*" Mary. She is always wanting us to depend on her and to steal Glory and Worship from Jesus and The Father.

CHAPTER 8
DISCERNING AN APPARITION

In the previous chapters we've seen how it's possible to confuse the *real* Mary with the *false* Mary and how important it is to discern all supernatural events. We must seek God and the Word of God and ask where the vision or apparition comes from.

One of the most common strategies satan uses to deceive us is with his false angels of light. The Bible is full of supernatural encounters with celestial beings but not everything that takes place in the spiritual atmosphere is of God.

One of the biggest errors occurs when we allow ourselves to be influenced by the beauty or light of an apparition, or by the name it uses to identify itself. These can be deceiving. as well as the miracles and wonders that come with it.

God is not the only one who performs miracles. Warlocks and sorcerers can perform works of healing and the devil himself can do them too, but he can't do all things. He does just enough to set his trap to capture us. The devil is a master illusionist and he creates all sorts of deceiving images to make us believe an image is from God because it weeps or bleeds.

For the mystery of lawlessness is already at work ...

... lawless one is according to the working of satan, with all power, signs, and lying wonders, and with all unrighteous deception among those who perish, because they did not receive the love of the truth, that they might be saved. And for this reason God will send them strong delusion, that they should believe the lie, that they all may be condemned who didn't believe the truth but had pleasure in unrighteousness.

2 Thessalonians 2a & 9-12

John the Apostle lived in Ephesus where many supernatural events took place. He instructed his disciples to discern all spirits.

Beloved, do not believe every spirit, but test the spirits, whether they are of God; because many false prophets have gone out into the world. By this you know the Spirit of God: Every spirit that confesses that Jesus Christ has come in the flesh is of God,

1 John 4:1-2

A spirit that comes from God will always give Glory to God and will recognize the Lordship of Jesus Christ. This means the message of a true messenger of God will always point to Jesus as the supreme authority under The Father. God has a clear message and satan has a clear message. Both messengers will be coherent and aligned with the message of the one they serve.

The Message from God

The message from God points to the Son and His work here on earth. His messengers are sent to give messages that align us to what Jesus did for us. God's message points to Jesus Christ and the salvation provided by Him. God's message leads man to repentance and its fruit is righteous lives that worship Him.

Jesus speaking of His messengers said: "Messengers are under authority"

Most assuredly, I say to you, a servant is not greater than his master; nor is he who is sent greater than he who sent him.

John 13:16

The message of Gabriel, the archangel to Mary: "The Kingship of Jesus Christ"

And behold, you will conceive in your womb and bring forth a Son, and shall call His name Jesus. He will be great, and will be called the Son of the Highest; and the Lord God will give Him the throne of His father David. And He will reign over the house of Jacob forever, and of His kingdom there will be no end."

Luke 1:31-33

The message of the nativity angels: "Jesus is The Savior"

Then the angel said to them, "Do not be afraid, for behold, I bring you good tidings of great joy which will be to all people. For there is born to you this day in the city of David a Savior, who is Christ the Lord.

Luke 2:10-11

Some messages from the Apostles: "Only through Jesus can one be saved." or "The temple of The Holy Spirit is our bodies."

Nor is there salvation in any other, for there is no other name under heaven given among men by which we must be saved.

Acts 4:12

Or do you not know that your body is the temple of the Holy Spirit who is in you, whom you have from God, and you are not your own? For you were bought at a price; therefore glorify God in your body and in your spirit, which are God's.

1 Corinthians 6:19-20

The Message from the devil

The devil, on the other hand, always wants to exalt himself and will do whatever he can to entice people to bow before him and worship him. He offered Jesus all of the kingdoms of the earth, riches and compensation. If he tempted Jesus Himself in this manner, what wouldn't he do with regular human beings that don't know what is written in the Word of God?

Again, the devil took Him up on an exceedingly high mountain, and showed Him all the kingdoms of the world and their glory. And he said to Him, "All these things I will give You if You will fall down and worship me."

Then Jesus said to him, "Away with you, satan! For it is written, 'You shall worship the Lord your God, and Him only you shall serve.'"

Matthew 4:8-10

Idolatry is the way the devil disguises himself in order to be worshipped. For this reason God detests it to the point where He calls it a spirit of fornication. God longs for and requires that He be the only one to be worshipped. God knows that when man begins to seek answers in figurines, paintings or metal works, His enemy the devil is behind it. God knows it will end up destroying the people He loves so much.

My people ask counsel from their wooden idols, and their staff informs them.

For the spirit of harlotry has caused them to stray, and they have played the harlot against their God. They offer sacrifices on the mountaintops, and burn incense on the hills, under oaks, poplars, and terebinths, because their shade is good. Therefore your daughters commit harlotry, and your brides commit adultery. "I will not punish your daughters when they commit harlotry, nor your brides when they commit adultery; for the men themselves go apart with harlots, And offer sacrifices with a ritual harlot. Therefore people who do not understand will be trampled.

Hosea 4:12-14

Keeping all of this in mind, let's analyze some of the messages from the supposed apparitions of Mary and see if it's the *real* mother of Jesus, or an apparition created by the devil.

1.) Analysis of the Virgin of Guadalupe

Fig. 42 — Apparition of the Virgin of Guadalupe to Juan Diego

In Mexico at the Mount of Tepeyac where the Aztecs worshipped the goddess Coatlaxope-Tonatzin, it's said the Virgin of Guadalupe appeared.

Here is the story and message from the Virgin of Guadalupe according to the accounts from the Basilica which bears her name.

"Before her, Juan Diego prostrated himself and heard the sweet and affable voice of Our Lady of Heaven, in the Mexican language, she said: 'Listen my son, the youngest, Juanito. Where are you headed?' And he answered: 'My Lady, Queen, My Young Lady, I will head over to your little house in Mexico Tlatilolco, to follow the things of God they give us, where our Priests teach us who the images of Our Lord are.' In this way, holding a dialogue with Juan Diego, the precious Maiden expressed who she was and what her will was.

"Know and understand well, you the most humble of my son, that I am the ever virgin Holy Mary, **Mother of the True God for whom we live, of the Creator of all things, the owner of intimacy and immediacy, Owner of heaven and of the earth**. Much I desire, much I wish that a **holy little house** will be erected here quickly, so I may therein exhibit and give all my love, compassion and help **through my salvation**; because I truly am your merciful mother, to you, and to all the inhabitants on this land and all other lineage of men who love me, invoke and confide in me; I will listen there to their lamentations, and to bring a remedy and a cure to all their miseries, afflictions and sorrows, and to accomplish what my compasionate look pretends. Go then to the palace of the bishop of Mexico, and you will say to him that I have manifested my great desire, that here on this plain a house, a temple be built to me; you will accurately relate all you have seen and admired, and what you have heard. Be assured that I will be most grateful and will repay you, because I will enrich you and glorify and you will be worthy of recompense for the effort and fatigue in what you will obtain of what I have entrusted."[10]

If we look closely at this message we'll find that it clearly points to the Mary we should attribute the apparition to — the *false* Mary.

a. This virgin calls herself the mother of the creator, the owner of heaven and earth, in other words she calls herself the mother of the very Heavenly Father.

b. Jesus, the Son of the *real* Mary and Savior of the World is not even mentioned.

---

[10] (*Translation from the original manuscript in the native language.*)
https://www.aciprensa.com/Maric/Guadalupe/nican.htm

c. She calls herself the savior of humanity, a title that only belongs to Jesus Christ for having taken our sin and death on the cross of Calvary.

d. She requests that a temple be built. A temple is only built for a god with the purpose of offering worship.

e. She offers Juan Diego a reward for his worship, the same thing satan offered Jesus during the temptation in the desert.

Here is a historic document where you can clearly see the mixture between Tonatzin, the Aztec goddess and the Spanish Guadalupana:

Fig. 43 — "It is "flower and song;" that is, prayers and poetic passages, written in a pre-Hispanic way, but in key Christian theology, as Jose Luis Guerrero Rosado analyzed and exhibited in his work with said title."[11]

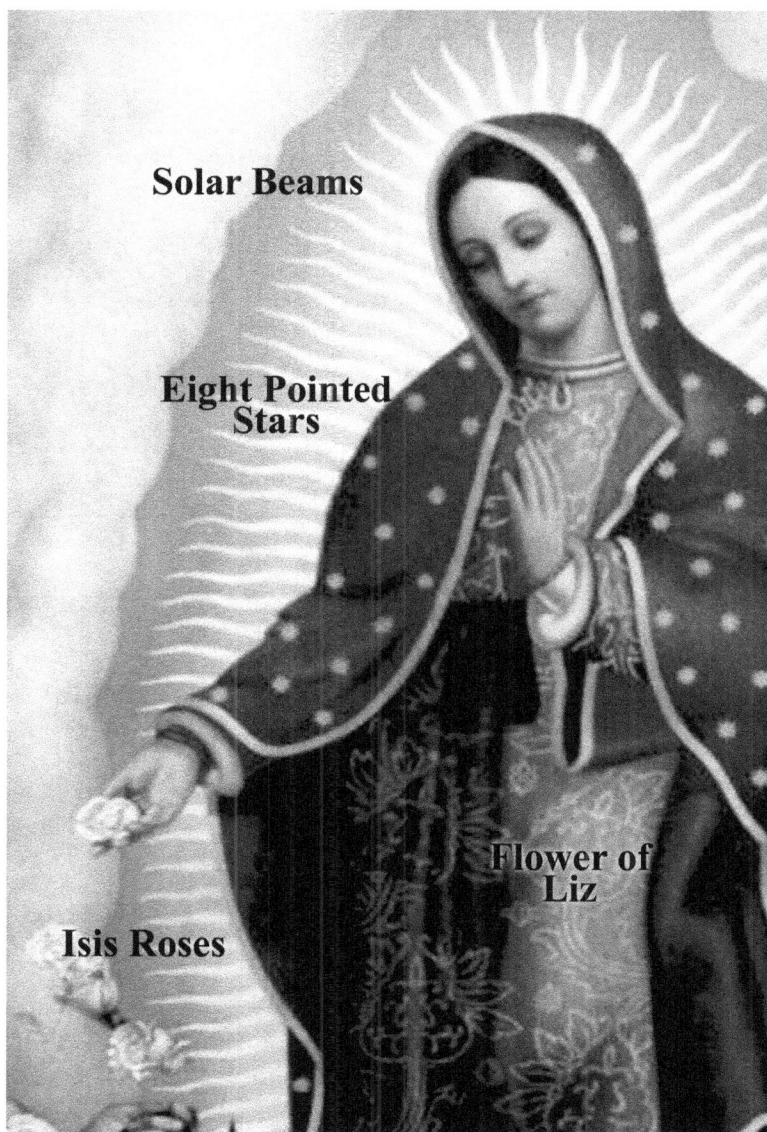

Solar Beams

Eight Pointed
Stars

Isis Roses

Flower of
Liz

Fig. 44 — Besides the syncretism or mixture of different beliefs or practices with the goddess Tonatzin, once again we can see Ishtar's, Isis and Venus' symbols in the Guadalupana's dress.

2.) Message from the Virgin of Fatima

Fig. 45 — Virgin with Children

The message from the Virgin of Fatima apparition to the three shepherds in Portugal is very long, so I will only include a portion to shed enough light to help discern the origin of this apparition. (The complete message is found in the *Appendix* and in *Footnote 11* of this Book):

"I am the Lady of the Rosary; continue praying the Rosary every day, the war will be over soon."

Here is the story and message of one of her apparitions:

"After this event, the clairvoyant children were very frightened and Our Lady spoke to them with goodness and sadness: 'Have you seen hell where many sinners will fall? **In order to save them, the Lord wants to establish the devotion of the Immaculate Heart of Mary on the earth. I have come to ask for the Consecration of the world to the heart of Mary** and the Communion of the First Saturdays for redress and repair for so many sins.'"[12]

This message clearly annuls Christ's sacrifice as the one and only sufficient plan for our salvation. This message is saying that Christ's death and resurrection are worthless when it comes to saving us. What this apparition proposes is to create a devotion to an image called, "Immaculate Heart of Mary."

Jesus made this very clear in the gospels:

a. Genuine repentance for our sins.

and (Jesus) saying, "The time is fulfilled, and the kingdom of God is at hand. Repent, and believe in the gospel."

Mark 1:15

---

[12] *http://www.rosary-center.org/fatimams.htm*

b. Believe in the gospel which announces the merits of Christ, His death, and resurrection as the way for our salvation.

And He said to them, "Go into all the world and preach the gospel to every creature. He who believes and is baptized will be saved; but he who does not believe will be condemned.

And these signs will follow those who believe: In My name they will cast out demons; they will speak with new tongues; they will take up serpents; and if they drink anything deadly, it will by no means hurt them; they will lay hands on the sick, and they will recover."

So then, after the Lord had spoken to them, He was received up into heaven, and sat down at the right hand of God. And they went out and preached everywhere, the Lord working with them and confirming the word through the accompanying signs. Amen.

Mark 16:15-20

c. Salvation is by grace and not by the works of man.

For by grace you have been saved through faith, and that not of yourselves; it is the gift of God, not of works, lest anyone should boast.

Ephesians 2:8-9

When we learn what Jesus did for us and we hear the messages of these apparitions, it becomes clear they could not have come from the *real* Mary, who honored and faithfully believed in what her Son did for humanity.

3.) The Message of the Virgin of Medjugorje

Fig. 46 — Virgin

This is one of the more recent apparitions that has manifested. Her message is the one I consider most difficult to discern, since she continuously mentions her son; however, she never identifies Him as Jesus Christ.

It's important to understand that being "*false*" is not the opposite of being "*real*". Being "false" actually contains a great deal of reality, but at some point it twists reality to obtain its fraudulent objective.

For instance, a counterfeit or false US$100-bill has many identical parts of the real one. It has the appearance of the real thing, but it doesn't come from the same source as the true bill.

I've taken certain portions of the message from this apparition to help discern its origin. If you want to read the entire message you may do so at the Medjugorge website (See Footnote 13).

"Beloved Children! I come among you because I desire to be your Mother and intercessor. **I desire to be the bond between you and your heavenly Father; your mediator.** I desire to take you in my hands and walk with you in the fight against this impure spirit. My children: **Consecrate yourselves totally to me. I will take your lives in my maternal hands** and will show you peace and love and then I will turn them over to My Son." I ask you to pray and fast because **that is the only way you can testify of My Son in the right way through my maternal Heart.** Pray for your pastors so that united in my Son you can always gladly announce the Word of God. I thank you."[13]

I highlighted the parts in bold type that clearly oppose the message and work of Jesus.

a. She proposes that she is the mediator between man and The heavenly Father.

---

[13] *http://www.medjugorje.ws/en/messages/*

The Bible says:

> *For there is one God and one Mediator between God and men, the Man Christ Jesus…*
>
> *1 Timothy 2:5*

b. She calls them to consecrate themselves *totally to her* so that she may take their lives in her hands.

The *real* Mary would never do such a thing! She knows scripture and she knows perfectly well that access to the Son is direct. Jesus Christ has no need for a mediator - especially one that requires lives be given to her instead. Mary was Hebrew and in Hebrews 4 the following is written:

> *Seeing then that we have a great High Priest who has passed through the heavens, Jesus the Son of God, let us hold fast our confession. For we do not have a High Priest who cannot sympathize with our weaknesses, but was in all points tempted as we are, yet without sin. Let us therefore come boldly to the throne of grace, that we may obtain mercy and find grace to help in time of need.*
>
> *Hebrews 4:14-16*

This was a brief, but accurate analysis of some of the messages from Mary's apparitions. It's clear that these are from the *false* Mary seeking our lives, as well as our worship.

CHAPTER 9

JESUS' POSITION AND
THE REAL MARY
IN OUR LIVES AS BELIEVERS

The truth is our Heavenly Father is not far away. Jesus said, "The Kingdom of God has come upon you." Jesus is real and He is alive. He is no longer hanging on the cross as we see Him in so many sculptures in churches. He is not a small child in someone's arms who lacks power. He was resurrected and He is seated at the right hand of The Father waiting for us to open our hearts and invite Him in so He can fill our lives and transform us.

Jesus wants to be our one and only sufficient Savior. He wants to cleanse our souls and give us eternal life so we can be seated by His side even while we are here on this earth; and not only when we depart to go be with Him.

The Good News of the gospel is not complicated. Jesus is alive and He wants us to have a marvelous relationship with Him. We don't need to spend our lives in a monastery or a convent to receive the great promises that Jesus left us. They can become a reality in our lives today.

If you love Me, keep My commandments. And I will pray the Father, and He will give you another Helper, that He may abide with you forever — the Spirit of truth, whom the world cannot receive, because it neither sees

Him nor knows Him; but you know Him, for He dwells with you and will be in you.

I will not leave you orphans; I will come to you. A little while longer and the world will see Me no more, but you will see Me. Because I live, you will live also.

At that day you will know that I am in My Father, and you in Me, and I in you. He who has My commandments and keeps them, it is he who loves Me. And he who loves Me will be loved by My Father, and I will love him and manifest Myself to him.

John 14:15-21

*If anyone loves Me, he will keep My word; and **My Father will love him, and We will come to him and make Our home with him.***

John 14:23

If you abide in Me, and My words abide in you, you will ask what you desire, and it shall be done for you.

John 15:7

These promises can become a reality now in our lives. The door to salvation is called Jesus Christ and in order to enter, we must consider the great price He paid on the cross for us. Then we must deeply repent of our sins and determine in our heart not to commit those sins again. At the start of our walk with Christ we may stumble and fall, but our determination should be to get up and try with all of our heart to remain in righteousness and holiness. The work does not depend on us. His redeeming grace will perfect anyone who desires to faithfully follow Him.

I invite you to close your eyes for a moment and reflect on your walk with God. If you want to make Jesus Christ your one and only sufficient Lord and Savior you may speak to your Heavenly Father with words from your heart or you can pray this prayer:

Prayer of Salvation

Lord Jesus, I come before You today, recognizing I am a sinner who needs salvation. I deeply repent for offending You - sometimes in my ignorance and at other times with full conviction of what I was doing. I recognize that the only way to be saved is through Your sacrifice on the cross. I receive Your sacrifice in which You died for me.

I renounce the spirit of the false Mary and every bond and pact I ever made with her.

I confess You today and always as my Lord and my God and my one and only sufficient Savior. My worship will be only for You, The Heavenly Father and The Holy Spirit.

I open my heart to You today so You may come and live in me. I give you my life, my heart, my thoughts and my body so You may be Lord of all. I ask You to fill me with The Holy Spirit so He may direct my steps and take me into all Truth.

In the Name of Jesus Christ, the King of Kings, Amen.

Relationship with the Real Mary

When Jesus was on the earth He never established a special relationship between us and His mother. Mary died and was taken to heaven where we will meet her when we are promoted to glory after leaving this earth.

Mary, however, deserves our respect and honor. As I said earlier, honoring her is not the same as worshipping her or performing ceremonial rituals to her. And we can't depend on her or pray to her. We must simply give her the rightful place as the most blessed among women and also as an anointed one of God.

> *Do not touch My anointed ones, And do My prophets no harm.*
>
> *Psalms 105:15*

Part of honoring Mary consists of separating her from the *false* Mary. May The Holy Spirit make it known to her in heaven that there are people who are making this distinction. Jesus understands how much suffering it must cause her to know that she is being confused with that abominable idol - none other than satan wanting to be just like The Most High.

To honor her is to learn from her immovable faith and her respect and worship to God The Father. By doing so, we will also be like Mary in her fear of offending Him.

Her life left us a very clear message and an unprecedented example to follow.

Her message is simple:

Let it be to me according to your word!
Whatever He says to you, do it!

Let it be to me according to your word!

May all the promises that Jesus and the Father left us be fulfilled in our lives and may we have the faith Mary had. She never wavered, but always believed.

May we not fear persecution if we are serving and following the Lord. His promises are greater than anything man can say or do to us.

May we never forget how low we are before the supreme Majesty of The Father. May we never cease to give thanks for the innumerable mercies of God.

May we always keep in mind that He chose us and we didn't choose Him. This makes us debtors. We must love Him and serve Him with all our heart _and_ we must also love one another.

> *You did not choose Me, but I chose you and appointed*
> *you that you should go and bear fruit, and that your*
> *fruit should remain, that whatever you ask the Father*
> *in My name He may give you. These things I*
> *command you, that you love one another.*
>
> *John 15:16-17*

Mary lived through one of the most intense pains ever, which was seeing her Son beaten, pierced and nailed to the cross.

If anyone lived the harrowing impact of the crucifixion it was Mary. She touched the fresh wounds when they lowered His body from the cross. It's those very wounds which carried all of our sins and infirmities.

> *He is despised and rejected by men, a Man of sorrows and acquainted with grief. And we hid, as it were, our faces from Him; He was despised, and we didn't esteem Him. Surely He has borne our griefs and carried our sorrows; Yet we esteemed Him stricken, smitten by God, and afflicted. But He was wounded for our transgressions, He was bruised for our iniquities; The chastisement for our peace was upon Him.*
>
> *Isaiah 53:3-5*

It's so marvelous to receive what Jesus did for us with the same faith Mary had when she said, *"Let it be to me according to your word,"* and to be healed and comforted by faith. May we live with the same impact of the cross that Mary lived and may we honor God in everything we do.

What honors Mary is that we live according to her Son, Jesus Christ.

Whatever He says to you, do it!

As Jesus also said, *"He who has My commandments and keeps them, it is he who loves Me."*

The problem with following idols is people grow accustomed to the fact that idols can't hear, see or speak spiritually. That's why a vast majority of people live their lives in any way they please and have no Fear of God. They hate each other and they sin against true love, violating His commandments without any remorse.

If we want to follow Mary's example we must draw near to God to be sanctified and trust in His redeeming grace, longing and seeking a greater purification.

CONCLUSION

I've been led by The Holy Spirit in writing this book. It's my desire to help bring light to those like me, who were deceived by the "false Mary, the Queen of Heaven." Very simply, not everything that shines is from heaven or comes from God. I hope and pray you will come to know the truth because then you will be set completely free as I have been blessed to be set free.

The journey does not end when you close these pages. In fact, it's just beginning! It's the responsibility of those of us who love God to take the truth to those who do not have it yet.

Join me and be a part of this great assignment God laid on my heart. May you share this book with someone who truly needs it.

WHAT'S NEXT?

The question for those who have now found this truth is what to do with any paintings and sculptures honoring the *false* Mary you have in your possession.

It's important to destroy these idols and remove them from your home since they are responsible for misfortune and disgrace. The Queen of Heaven specifically uses suffering, poverty and sickness, so people cling to her. And, therefore, idols to her also produce suffering, poverty and sickness.

The poorest countries with the most corruption and suffering are those consecrated to the *false* Mary and have her as their patron saint.

God is not seeking your suffering so you seek Him. He loves you and His thoughts are for blessings and continuous well-being for those who love Him and follow Him.

> *For I know the thoughts that I think toward you, says the Lord, thoughts of peace and not of evil, to give you a future and a hope.*
>
> *Jeremiah 29:11*

However, do you recall the message from the same Prophet Jeremiah to the people of Israel when they worshipped the Queen of Heaven?

> *Now therefore, thus says the Lord, the God of hosts, the God of Israel: 'Why do you commit this great evil against yourselves...?*
>
> *Jeremiah 44:7*

God tells us in His word specifically what to do with these sculptures and paintings:

> *You shall burn the carved images of their gods with fire; you shall not covet the silver or gold that is on them, nor take it for yourselves, lest you be snared by it; for it is an abomination to the Lord your God.*
>
> *Deuteronomy 7:25*

And you shall destroy their altars, break their sacred pillars, and burn their wooden images with fire; you shall cut down the carved images of their gods and destroy their names from that place.

Deuteronomy 12:3

The great fear most people feel after burning these images is because they think they are committing some sort of sacrilege. In reality, that fear which comes over them is directly from the Queen of Heaven. She refuses to leave those people because she wants to prevent them from living a righteous life before God.

As a matter of fact, if the *real* Mary could speak to us she would be very happy to know that we have disassociated her from that demon.

Just as she said of her Son, *"Whatever He says to you, do it."*

Therefore in prayer, ask God to cover you with the Blood of Jesus and trust that His protection is infinite.

If you must destroy items made of gold, you may melt them, but don't covet the gold for yourselves. Give it to the poor or to someone in need. If it's a valuable work of art, place your trust in God and love Him more than that image. When you take a step like this, God Himself will restore the loss with a great financial miracle or with a more valuable work of art that does not offend Him.

Once this is done, you are ready to begin the greatest walk there is with Jesus Christ, The Father and The Holy Spirit.

Now, begin reading the Bible because it will light your path. It may be better to start with the New Testament because it's easier to understand. Always ask The Holy Spirit to speak to you, guide you and instruct you in all truth.

Ask The Lord to surround you with people who know Him - people who will be a blessing to your spiritual lives.

I bless you now with every blessing from above so that all goes well with you and you have abundant health and prosper as your soul prospers.

"Beloved, I pray that you may prosper in all things and be in health, just as your soul prospers."

3 John 1:2

APPENDIX: VIRGIN OF FATIMA

Since the May 13, 1917 the Virgin Mary appeared six times to three young shepherds: Lucia, Francisco and Jacinta in Fatima (a town in Portugal north of Lisbon).

We recommend you read, "Memories of Lucia" for more information. She is one of the three children who saw the virgin and she recounts the details of these apparitions in her book.

First Apparition: May 13, 1917

The following dialogue took place on May 13th:

"Where are you from?"

"Heaven is my home."

"And what do you want from us?"

"I want to ask you to return here on the 13th of each month at the very same hour (noon). In October I shall tell you who I am, and what it is that I most desire."

"And shall we go to heaven?"

"Lucia and Jacinta will."

"And Francisco?"

The apparition's eyes turned to the young man. She had an expression of goodness and maternal reproach and said:

"He too shall go to heaven, but he will first have to pray many Rosaries."

She continued, "Are you willing to offer yourselves to God, and bear all the sufferings He sends you in atonement for all the sins that offend Him?"

"Yes, we are willing and we accept."

With a gesture of happiness after seeing their generosity, she said:

"Then you will have a great deal to suffer, but the grace of God will be with you and will strengthen you."

Second Apparition: June 13, 1917

The virgin tells the three children, "It's important that you pray the Rosary every day, and learn to read."

Lucia asks her for the healing of a sick person and the virgin says, "If he converts, he will be healed within a year."

Lucia supplicates: "I would like to ask you to take us to heaven."

"Yes, I will take Jacinta and Francisco soon, but you are to stay here longer. Jesus wishes to make use of you to make me known and loved. He wants to establish devotion in the world to my Immaculate Heart."

"Am I to stay here alone in this world?"

"No, my daughter! Are you suffering a great deal? Don't lose heart, I will never forsake you. My Immaculate Heart will be your refuge and the way that will lead you to God."

Third Apparition: July 13th, 1917

There were 4,000 people. Our lady said to the seers: "It's necessary to pray the Rosary so that the war will end. Praying to the virgin can bring peace. When you suffer say: 'Oh Jesus, it's for your love and for the conversion of sinners.'"

The virgin opened her hands and a beam of light penetrated the earth. An enormous furnace full of fire appeared and in it were people that looked like burning embers that were brought to the top by flames and would then fall screaming amid groans of pain. Lucia screamed in fear. The children lifted their eyes towards the virgin as if asking for help and She said:

"Have you seen hell where so many sinners will fall? In order to save them, the Lord wants to establish devotion to the Immaculate Heart of Mary. If prayer and penitence are made, many souls will be saved and peace will come. But, if there is no prayer and sin does not cease, another war will come even worse than the ones before, and the punishment of the world for its sins will be war, famine, and the persecution of the Holy Church and the Holy Father.

I have come to ask for the Consecration of the world to the Heart of Mary and for Communion on the first Saturday of every month in atonement and repair for so many sins. If what I am requesting is accepted, peace will come, but if it's not accepted an erroneous godless propaganda will spread throughout the world and there will be wars and persecution of the church. Many good people will be martyred and the Holy Father will suffer greatly. Several nations will be destroyed, but in the end my Immaculate Heart will triumph."

Our Lady added: "When you pray the Rosary, after every mystery say: 'O my Jesus, forgive us, save us from the fire of hell. Lead all souls to heaven, especially those who are most in need.'"

Fourth Apparition: August 1917

The Fourth Apparition didn't take place on August 13th because the mayor held the three children in prison to get them to deny that they had seen the virgin. He didn't succeed. The apparition took place a few days later.

The virgin said in the Fourth Apparition: "Pray, pray very much and make sacrifices for sinners. You must remember that many souls are being condemned because there is no one that will pray and make sacrifices for them". (Pope Pius XII would say that this phrase was the one that would impress him the most from Fatima's message and would exclaim: "Tremendous mystery: that the salvation of many souls depends on the prayers and sacrifices that are made for sinners).

Since this apparition the three children dedicated themselves to offering as many sacrifices as possible for the conversion of sinners and began to pray the Rosary with fervor.

Fifth Apparition: September 13, 1917

There were now 12,000 people. Our Lady recommended to the seers that they continue praying the Rosary and she announced the end of the war. Lucia asks her for several sick people. The virgin says that some would be healed and that others would not because God didn't trust them. She also said that for the sanctification of some people, sickness was more convenient than health. She invited everyone to participate in a great miracle on October 13th.

Sixth and Final Apparition: October 13, 1917

There were now 70,000 people. The apparition said to the three children: "I am the Virgin of the Rosary. I want a chapel built here in my honor. I want you to continue saying the Rosary every day."

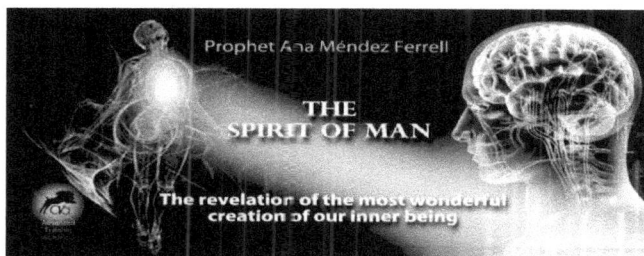

Voice Of The Light Ministries

www.voiceofthelight.com

904-834-2447

P.O. Box 3418

Ponte Vedra, FL 32004

USA